Berg Women's Series

General Editor: MIRIAM KOCHAN

Gertrude Bell	SUSAN GOODMAN
Mme De Staël	RENEE WINEGARTEN
Emily Dickinson	DONNA DICKENSON

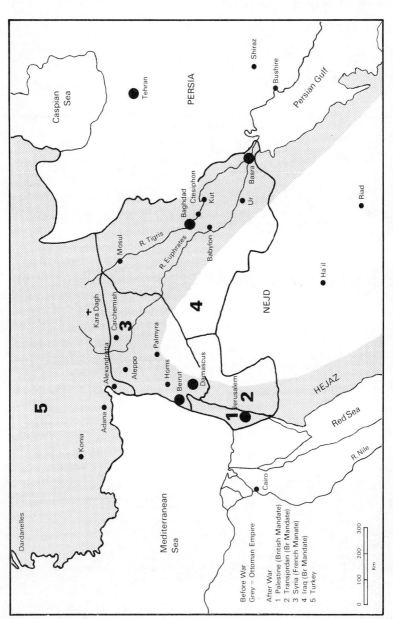

The Near East, showing the main cities (ancient and modern) referred to in this book.

Before War
Grey = Ottoman Empire

After War
1 Palestine (British Mandate)
2 Transjordan (Br Mandate)
3 Syria (French Manate)
4 Iraq (Br Mandate)
5 Turkey

Km
0   100   200   300

Gertrude Bell

Susan Goodman

BERG *Leamington Spa/Dover NH/Heidelberg*

© copyright Berg Publishers 1985

British Library Cataloguing in Publication Data

Goodman, Susan
   Gertrude Bell.—(Berg women's series)
   1. Bell, Gertrude   2. Travelers—East—
   Biography
   I. Title
   915'.0441'0924   G463.B42

ISBN 0 907582 86 9
    0 907582 68 0 (pbk)

Library of Congress Cataloging-in-Publication Data
Goodman, Susan.
   Gertrude Bell.

   (Berg women's series)
   Bibliography: p
   1. Bell, Gertrude Lowthian, 1868–1926.
2. Orientalists—Biography.   3. Colonial administrators
—Great Britain—Biography.   4. Colonial administrators—
Near East—Biography.   1. Title.   II. Series.
DS61.7.B37G66   1985   956.9'0072024 [B]   85–15024

Published in 1985 by **Berg Publishers Ltd**,
24 Binswood Avenue, Leamington Spa, CV32 5SQ, UK
51 Washington Street,
Dover, New Hampshire 03820, USA
Panoramastr. 118,
6900 Heidelberg, West Germany

Printed by Billing & Sons, Worcester

Contents

Illustrations

Introduction

On the evening of 12 July 1926 there was a great public funeral in Baghdad. Thousands of Arabs followed the coffin of Gertrude Bell to the British cemetery on the outskirts of the city. She had died that morning from an overdose of a sleeping potion, just two days before her fifty-eighth birthday. She was deeply mourned by the princes and people of Iraq and eulogized by her own king and country.

During her lifetime the name of Gertrude Bell evoked for the British rich images of the exotic and mysterious Arab world. But her fame faded fast and now most of us only remember her eccentric friend and colleague, T. E. Lawrence.

She was born into one of the richest and most enlightened industrial families in Britain and flourished in its intellectual freedom. At the age of seventeen her parents decided 'with some qualms' to send her to Lady Margaret Hall in Oxford, which had opened just seven years before. After only five terms, instead of the usual three years, she took a first class honours degree in modern history.

In the years following Oxford she travelled widely and often unconventionally, showing immense physical courage when journeying alone through the hostile, sun-baked deserts of the Middle East or scaling testing peaks in the Swiss Alps. Her life brought emotional as well as physical tests and in these years she twice suffered the tragedy of love ended by death.

But it was as a British political officer in Baghdad that she most drew on her mental, physical and emotional resources to exert considerable influence in determining the future of fragments of the Ottoman empire; and it was Mesopotamia, later to be called Iraq, that won her heart and mind, and finally claimed her body.

The Iraqis called her 'al-Khatun', which the English translated as 'The Lady'. The name meant much more in Arabic: she was 'The Lady of the court', a recognition of her social and political status, and her commitment to the Arabs. But Gertrude Bell was also a 'lady' in the Victorian sense of the word. She had the charm, manners and dress of a lady of Victorian society. She

1

had been nurtured by a successful and confident Victorian family and retained its style and standards even among the sheikhs of the desert and the vicissitudes of Arab politics.

Fortunately for her biographer Gertrude's life is extremely well documented. Her travels in the desert are recorded in the books she wrote: travelogues and detailed archaeological treatises. Information and recommendations relating to political developments and intrigue in the crumbling Ottoman Empire are contained in the reports she wrote for the British government when working as political secretary for the Arab Bureau in Mesopotamia. The details of her everyday life are found in her diaries and letters to her father and stepmother. These letters were preserved by the Bell family; several volumes of them have been published. Today her entire correspondence and the hundreds of photographs she took on her travels, are preserved in an archive at the University of Newcastle-upon-Tyne.

Her letters are written in a delightful, free-flowing style, and reading them alone is enough to bring you close to the spirit of Gertrude Bell. It has been my task to place her life in the context of the times in which she lived. Her life story weaves its way through major social and political developments in Victorian Britain; it takes us to the front line in the First World War, the battlefields of Gallipoli, and to the turbulent birth of nations in the Middle East.

1 Caterpillar to Butterfly

On 14 July 1868, at the Hall in the small village of Washington in County Durham, a daughter, Gertrude Margaret Lowthian, was born to Hugh and Mary Bell. She belonged to one of England's leading industrial families and had been given the name of its most illustrious member, her grandfather, Lowthian Bell.

Lowthian was the source of his family's considerable and increasing fortune. He had followed his father into the iron industry and had become an unrivalled authority on the scientific principles of the blast-furnace. His scientific education made him unique among the industrialists of Britain at that time. In the 1850s he had established the foundations of the Cleveland iron and steel industry, setting up the blast-furnaces of the Clarence works on the bank of the river Tees opposite the new industrial town of Middlesbrough. Here industry expanded, and by the mid-1870s Cleveland was producing one-third of the output of British iron.

Cleveland, like other new industrial developments in the provinces, was under the control of a rising upper-middle class, which had benefited from the growth in free trade — the first tariffs being lifted by Peel's budget of 1842. And then in the late 1860s they began to gain real political power. The 1867 Reform Bill enfranchised some of the new industrial urban communities and the character of Parliament changed. Prior to the Bill it was noted that well over half of the Members of Parliament formed a 'cousinhood' of landed families. At the general election of 1868, the year of Gertrude's birth, Lowthian Bell contested the seat for North Durham. He lost, but in 1875 took his seat as a Liberal Member of Parliament for the Hartlepools.

Gertrude was born at a time when the Bells' wealth and prestige were rising fast. Before she was three the family had added two new splendid residences to their estates: Redbarns at Redcar, on the Yorkshire coast, belonged to her father Hugh Bell and Rounton Grange at nearby Northallerton was built for Lowthian. Both houses were designed by the architect Philip Webb, the friend of William Morris. At Rounton, one of Webb's

3

most ambitious projects, the interior decoration was supervised by Morris himself. It became the centre of Bell family life until 1926, when it was abandoned and became derelict because of failing family fortunes. The Cleveland ironmasters had ceased to prosper. In the latter decades of the nineteenth century they were already succumbing to the effects of fierce competition from Germany and the USA; but before that, in the 1870s, when the rest of British industry was experiencing a 'great depression' the modern industries of Cleveland were virtually unscathed. During the years of Gertrude's childhood and youth her family enjoyed almost continuous prosperity, and she enjoyed all the benefits that wealth could bring. But money could not protect her from the tragedies of life.

At the age of two Gertrude was dressed in black, the first of many such occasions in her life. She was mourning the death of her mother Mary, who had died of pneumonia three weeks after giving birth to her second child, Maurice Hugh Lowthian. A wet-nurse was found for Maurice, and Hugh Bell retreated to his new house at Redcar. Gertrude and Maurice came under the watchful eye of a German governess. But the firm authority of Miss Klug was soon to be tempered by gentler, more maternal care. In 1877 Hugh married again. His new wife, Florence, was highly cultured and accomplished; a respected playwright and always regarded as a 'perfect lady' by Victorian society.

Florence's father, Sir Joseph Olliffe, had been physician to the British Embassy in Paris and the family enjoyed a lavish life there, funded by his wife's fortune. He died in 1869 having invested a great deal of family money in an unremunerative project for the development of Deauville. Lady Olliffe and her children had been forced to flee Paris with the Prussian invasion of 1870 and returned to England, setting up home at 95 Sloane Street in London.

From the beginning Florence and Gertrude were friends. They first met when Gertrude was just six and Florence, then twenty-two, was introduced into the family as a friend of Hugh's sisters. Soon Gertrude began writing letters to 'my dear Florence' signed 'your affectionate little friend', and after her father's marriage the correspondence, now addressed to 'my dear mother', continued for the rest of her life. Gertrude wrote at least one letter a week, sometimes daily, from her school in London, from Lady Mar-

Gertrude Bell, aged 8, with her father, painted by Sir Edward Poynter.

garet Hall in Oxford, during her travels in Europe, and from remote deserts while on expedition. The letters show a close and loving relationship with family and also reveal Florence's influence on her stepdaughter, especially in matters of social etiquette.

Florence was well known for her dress-sense and good manners; Gertrude's Oxford friend, Janet Courtney, thought Florence 'so perfectly courteous, so socially accomplished; had a keen eye for lapses in good manners and refused to regard them as unimportant'. Her eye was at its most keen when observing Gertrude. Great importance was given to the presence of a suitable chaperon on any of Gertrude's outings from school, and later from her college in Oxford. Florence's sense of propriety probably went beyond contemporary concern. Gertrude wrote from Oxford:

Coming back from the cathedral I met Horace [Gertrude's cousin] with whom I strolled round the Parks and subsequently on to Merton. I hope you don't mind. Miss Wordsworth [the formidable principal of Lady Margaret Hall] says he may take me for little discreet (*sic*) walks every now and then. Please don't say you mind.

Sometimes the conventions of the day clearly irritated Gertrude: and she wrote home from her London school:

I wish I could go to the National, but you see there is no one to take me. If I were a boy, I should go to that incomparable place every week, but being a girl to see lovely things is denied to me.

She was subsequently reprimanded by Florence for referring to the 'National' by anything less than its full title of 'National Art Gallery'. The free-flowing, casual style that is now admired in Gertrude's letters was often criticized by her stepmother. Gertrude remained unaffected by Florence's pedantry and retained her own style of letter-writing and often her own style of spelling. But Florence was able to exercise considerable control over all other aspects of Gertrude's life. She carefully vetted the families of Gertrude's school friends before an invitation to lunch could be accepted. Even her reading was censored. Gertrude, aged twenty-three, wrote to her stepmother: 'Of course send back the

Disciple. I asked for it a long time ago but naturally I should have asked you about it before I read it'. The book was an immensely popular novel by Paul Bourget, which had sold 20,000 copies in the first weeks of publication. Perhaps the seduction of a maidservant rendered the book unsuitable.

Florence always ensured that her family was seen to conform to the highest standards of social etiquette. The Bells were trying to secure their position in the upper-middle class; they could easily afford the life-style of the upper classes but their ancestry and industry excluded them. Only marriage into aristocracy could provide the social status that *nouveaux riches* families craved for. Hugh Bell's sister Maisie made that social leap by marrying Lyulph Stanley, heir to the baronies of Alderley and Sheffield. His mother Lady Stanley 'always considered herself very broad-minded because she had not objected to Lyulph marrying into what she called "trade"'. Bertrand Russell, grandson of Lady Stanley, comments 'as Sir Hugh was a multi-millionaire I was not very much impressed'.

Shaking off the label 'trade' was easier for the next generation: the boys of the family, Gertrude's brothers and cousins, were educated at Eton and then usually went up to Oxford; the girls were educated at home, perfecting, with the help of governess and tutor, 'accomplishments' such as needlework and piano-playing. But Gertrude's conspicuous intellectual abilities presented problems to her family; she loathed playing the piano and filled her days with reading. She wrote in 1882 to her cousin Horace at Eton listing her week's reading:

Monday (evening) Mrs. Carlisle's letters. 1st vol.
Tuesday. Mrs. C's letters finished, began life of Macaulay.
Wednesday. I vol. Life of M. finished, began II vol.
Thursday II vol. Life of M. finished, I vol. Mozart's Letters finished. II vol. M's Letters began.
Friday II vol. M's Letters finished.
That is not bad is it? all these books are great fat ones . . . .
Now for something that will interest you more. Our collection of eggs is getting on splendidly.
P.S. Just tell me in your next if you could read this letter.

Gertrude's parents were finally persuaded to send her away, at the age of sixteen, to study at Queen's College in London. The school had been set up in 1848, developing from a series of 'Lectures for Ladies' given the previous year by the author Charles Kingsley and a few professors at King's College, part of London University. Queen's College was founded by a group of Christian Socialists who insisted that the school should provide an education based on Christian principles. It had quickly gained a good academic reputation. But in the 1880s it was still very unusual for an upper-middle class family to send a daughter away for schooling. The Bells had been persuaded by the new Lady President of Queen's College, Camilla Croudace. She was a close childhood friend of Gertrude's mother, Mary, and had asked the Bells to commit Gertrude to her care.

When Gertrude first went to Queen's College she stayed with Florence's mother, Lady Olliffe. After a year she became a boarder. These years were her first introduction to London society. Many of her stepmother's London friends invited Gertrude to their homes. One of the first invitations came from Mrs Richmond Ritchie, daughter of Thackeray, whose circle included the leading actresses, artists and writers of the day.

Gertrude's first visit clearly shook her self-esteem:

It is a very disagreeable process finding out that one is no better than the common run of people. I've gone through rather a hard course of it since I came to College and I don't like it at all; still I am afraid there is a great deal more to come.

It was not often that Gertrude felt loss of self-confidence. She generally held herself in high regard and it was this aspect of her character that in later years made her such a formidable Oriental Secretary in the Mesopotamian High Commission. She always had clear opinions which she clung to with great tenacity. While at school she already showed political acuity and a firm allegiance to the Liberal Party. Even during the political crisis in the years following 1885, when her father left the Liberals and joined the Liberal Unionists, Gertrude remained loyal to Gladstone. The crisis which had divided many Liberal families was brought about by Gladstone's dramatic shift of policy on Ireland. The Irish nationalists held the balance of power in Parliament for much of this period and in summer 1885 they voted with the

Conservative opposition, bringing down Gladstone's government. After the election the Conservatives took power, with Lord Salisbury as Prime Minister, but they needed the Irish vote to maintain a majority over the Liberals in Parliament. Then came the surprise that shook the Liberal Party. Gladstone gave support to Irish nationalist demands for Home Rule. The Irish Members of Parliament led by Parnell, deserted the Conservatives and allied themselves with the Liberals. Lord Salisbury's government fell and in February 1886 Gladstone became Prime Minister for the third time.

Shortly before his downfall in June 1885, Gladstone nominated Gertrude's grandfather, Lowthian Bell, for a baronetcy. Gertrude's Liberal principles were affronted and she wrote to Florence:

> I know about Grandpapa. I have written to congratulate him. I mayn't say to anyone else but I may say to you I suppose that I am very sorry indeed, it's a great pity. I think he quite deserves to have it only I wish it could have been offered and refused.

In later years Gertrude's father was more than once offered a peerage which he did refuse. At least in this he would gain Gertrude's approval if not on the subject of Irish Home Rule. Although there was never serious disagreement between them over the subject, it was the only issue in which there ever appeared a glimmer of difference of opinion between Gertrude and her father; in all other things his judgement and his decisions were accepted unquestioningly.

Many letters to her father and stepmother contain frank testimonies of her devotion to them and when Gertrude was sent to Queen's College in London she suffered dreadful homesickness. But her whole school life brightened as she became enthralled by the subject of modern history. She wrote in 1885 informing her stepmother that the school's history tutor, Mr de Soyres

> said in lecture that there was one paper which was the best he ever had given to him at College, and I made Miss Croudace say that it was mine — mine! He says it is most excellent, capital. Oh I'm so happy. He says I've a great deal of historic ability.

Soon Gertrude was writing to her father about plans for her future: 'Please I don't want you to tell anyone, not even mother. . . I have a burning ambition to go to Girton to read history'. She soon changed her mind: 'I've found just the very place for me. I'm not going to Girton but to Lady Margaret College (*sic*). Miss Croudace knows all about it and it must be delightful . . . fancy to be lectured by Freeman and Bright'. But her parents had their doubts. Her stepmother wrote years later: 'The time had not yet come when it was a usual part of a girl's education to go to University and it was with some qualms that we consented'.

A few months later Gertrude joined the college of her choice, Lady Margaret Hall in Oxford. It had been founded only seven years earlier and was the first of the women's colleges in Oxford. In Cambridge, Girton had been opened in 1872. The two colleges had very different characters at this time and it is not surprising that Miss Croudace should favour Lady Margaret Hall. Girton was uncompromising in its intellectual aims whereas Lady Margaret Hall reflected its Anglican foundation and preached the value of 'Christian virtues'. Its first principal, the devout Miss Elizabeth Wordsworth, great-niece of the poet William Wordsworth, had uncompromising views on the position of women in society: 'the creation of Eve gives the relation between the sexes as God intended them to be . . . she is Adam's helpmate'.

Miss Wordsworth insisted on greater attention to the 'minor graces' such as 'neat handwriting, skillful needlework and the way of opening and shutting doors'. She was especially concerned that 'if a girl has always got her head in a book, how are we to expect her when grown up to have a quick eye for the personal well-being of those around her'.

It is hardly surprising that Miss Wordsworth did not like the studious, non-religious Gertrude with her scrawling handwriting. 'Would she be the sort of person to have in one's bedroom if one were ill?' commented Miss Wordsworth.

The girls at Lady Margaret Hall did not spend their time attending to the 'minor graces'. They took their studies very seriously and obviously wanted to prove their intellectual worth in a society that for the most part refused to accept the value of higher education for women. The fact that the Bells allowed Gertrude to embark on university education reveals them as a

Lady Margaret Hall, 1888. Miss Wordsworth is in the centre, wearing a cap, with Gertrude Bell second on her left, in profile. Janet Hogarth is standing behind Gertrude.

highly enlightened family. The whole subject of women's higher education was a 'vexed and burning question of the day'. There was real concern that intense mental activity was unsuitable for the 'frail' female constitution. The philosopher Herbert Spencer made a clear statement of the commonly-held fears:

> Though the regimen of upper-class girls is better than that of girls belonging to the poorer classes, while, in most respects, their physical treatment is not worse, the deficiency of reproductive power among them may be reasonably attributed to the overtaxing of their brains which produces a serious reaction on the physique.

These ideas were fiercely contested in 1890 with the publication of Mrs H. Sidgwick's *Health Statistics of Women Students of Cambridge and Oxford and of their Sisters*. This showed that college-educated women did not have smaller families than their sisters — their reproductive power was unaffected by education.

When Gertrude went up to Oxford in early 1886 the position of women in the university was steadily improving. Two years earlier a statute had been passed allowing women to take men's examinations in modern history. But the 1884 statute had caused a great stir in the university: Dean Burgon preaching in New College Chapel regarded it as a 'reversal of the law of Nature which is also the law of God governing women . . . inferior to us God made you, and inferior to the end of time you will remain'.

Fortunately the women in Oxford had many friends in the university who allowed them to attend their lectures and arranged tutorials for them. And in Gertrude's first term her dream of being 'lectured by Freeman and Bright' was fulfilled. But the brilliance of Oxford did nothing to shake her self-confidence; she wrote to her stepmother about Freeman's lecture: 'He didn't say much about architecture, and what he did say wasn't true I thought.'

Lectures by Bright also provoked comment from Gertrude:

We went the other day to a lecture of Bright's. Bright didn't like having us at all — he met us with a very cross face and put us in seats with our backs turned to him . . . . As a rule we have a table to ourselves on the platform, but Bright wouldn't have us so near I think!

Gertrude thrived at Oxford, revelling in the academic and social life there. She was younger and much wealthier than most of the other girls at Lady Margaret Hall and was remembered by her college friend, Janet Courtney, as 'the most brilliant creature who ever came amongst us'.

After just five terms, instead of the usual nine, Gertrude took first class honours in modern history; a degree was never conferred upon her; that right was not won by women in Oxford until 1920. An account of Gertrude's viva voce at her finals examination was recorded by Janet Courtney:

At this oral examination Gertrude told her examiner Professor S.R. Gardiner, leading authority on the early Stuart period, 'I fear I don't quite agree with your view of Charles I'.

Gertrude's self-confidence bordered on arrogance and when she left Oxford her stepmother's sister Mary, wife of Sir Frank Lascelles the British minister in Bucharest, suggested that Gertrude join them in Romania 'to get rid of her Oxfordy manner'.

Gertrude's life in Bucharest was filled with dancing and polite conversation. During the fifteen months she spent there she met many diplomats who would rise to positions of great power: Prince Bülow, who became German imperial chancellor in 1900; Count Goluchowski, appointed minister of foreign affairs in Austria in 1895; Mr Hardinge, who was appointed Viceroy of India during the First World War and was responsible for sending Gertrude to the Arab Bureau in Basra in Mesopotamia. She also made the acquaintance of Valentine Chirol, soon to become foreign editor at *The Times*; he became a life-long friend and confidant.

After Bucharest followed a brief visit to Constantinople and then in 1889 Gertrude returned to England. For the next three years her life consisted of little more than marking time among family and friends. She extended her circle of 'intimates' in London to include 'the Russells of Audley Square whose home was a centre of social and intellectual life. Lord Arthur Russell was a son of the 6th Duke of Bedford, his wife was a gifted and brilliant Frenchwoman'; their daughter Flora became one of Gertrude's closest friends. The Norman Grosvenors were also among Gertrude's intimates, he 'very musical, a son of Lord Ebury, she, painting delightfully, a daughter of Right Hon. James Stuart Wortley'. The above descriptions of Gertrude's intimates, given years later by her sister, Elsa, was surely written to ensure that none of us is left in any doubt that Gertrude had definitely become a member of élite London society. She might have spent the rest of her life drifting among its brighter lights, but lying dormant among Gertrude's social graces was a spirit for adventure and romance — it would soon begin to stir.

2 Persian Pleasures

In July 1891 Gertrude received the news that the Lascelles were moving to Tehran. Her uncle Frank had been appointed British minister there. She wrote to her friend Flora Russell: 'My uncle goes to Persia in October, my aunt later. I don't know when. I should like her to take me out with her, Persia is the place I have always longed to see'.

In April 1892 Gertrude joined her aunt Mary and cousin Florence when they left England for the month's journey to Tehran. The delay between her uncle Frank's arrival and that of the rest of his family was probably due to anxiety over the tobacco protests that had spread through Persia since the spring of 1891. The unrest stemmed from the Shah's decision, influenced by the British minister in Tehran, to give a British company a monopoly over the production, sale and export of all Persian tobacco. The deal, which had been concluded in March 1890, was kept secret for almost a year but once it became public there were massive protests. Tobacco was grown throughout Persia and the new concession threatened the livelihood of local people. The religious authorities in Persia maintained that if the crop was under the exclusive control of non-Muslims then the product would be unfit for Muslim use. The protest culminated in a nation-wide boycott on the sale and use of tobacco and the Shah was forced to cancel the British concession. This was the beginning of a decline in British influence in Persia in favour of the Russians who had given some support to the tobacco protests.

Gertrude records the anti-British feeling that mounted towards the end of her stay in Persia. In September 1892 she wrote:

> The Mollahs are making great efforts to stir up the people against Ferengis [foreigners]. There is a rumour that they have forbidden all Persians to serve us . . . . The poor dear Nawab [one of the oriental secretaries in the British Legation] who is as good a Mussulman as the best of them, and may be seen any evening at the hour of prayer kneeling on a priceless carpet and bowing his head on a little piece of Mecca mud, has even been denounced by name for living with us.

Gertrude was fascinated by the culture of Persia — so different from anything she had ever experienced before. She described the landscape as if it were paradise, and she relished the beauty of the Persian language. She had spent the months in England before leaving for Persia studiously learning the language. When staying in the family house in Redcar Gertrude taught herself but while in London she had lessons and received many offers of help, including an unexpected visit one day from Lord Henry Stanley, the Muslim brother of uncle Lyulph Stanley. She also records yet 'another offer of lessons . . . I feel I shall end by receiving lessons from the Shah himself'. On arrival in Tehran she immediately found a teacher: a sheikh who came 'in a black astrachan hat and a brown collarless dressing gown over a white robe, and he sits with his hands folded and teaches Persian through the medium of very curious French'.

She quickly acquired fluency in Persian and began to read poems by the fourteenth-century mystical Sufi poet, Hafiz. For many years she worked on her own translation of his poems and in 1897 *Poems from the Divan of Hafiz* was published; it included a lengthy introduction on the life and times of Hafiz. The book won immediate acclaim and her translation was described in E.G. Browne's authoritative *Literary History of Persia* as 'probably the finest and most truly poetical renderings of any Persian poet ever produced in the English language'. The poems are not easily understood by the non-Muslim. Gertrude's extensive footnotes interpret many of the poems for us, though occasionally she 'found no explanation for these difficult lines'. For the Muslim, the *Divan of Hafiz* is not just a collection of poems; it is a source of mystical inspiration and is used, even today, for divination. The book is opened at random and the page pricked with a pin; the verse thus indicated is used as a source of advice or omen. Gertrude's interest in translating Hafiz's poems was primarily an intellectual exercise, but she was a romantic and no doubt found alluring the enigmatic verses alluding to love and death:

> My heart, sad hermit, stains the cloister floor
> With drops of blood, the sweat of anguish dire;
> Ah, wash me clean, and o'er my body pour
> Love's generous wine! the worshippers of fire
> Have bowed them down and magnified my name,

> For in my heart there burns a living flame,
> Transpiercing Death's impenetrable door.

She began translating Persian poetry within a month of arriving in Tehran. She wrote to her father about some early attempts at translating a thirteenth-century Sufi poet:

> There are some charming verses by Sadi which Mr Cadogan and I have been amusing ourselves by translating. His mistress gave him a piece of scented clay, he says, he asked it where it got the ambergris and musk which ravished his heart:
> "He answered me: Of clay I was and worthless
> Til by a rose I lay and breathed her sweetness".

The romance of the poetry reflected the love that was growing between Gertrude and Mr Cadogan. He was a secretary at the Embassy in Tehran, aged thirty-three and grandson of the third Earl of Cadogan. Gertrude had met him just a few days after arriving in Tehran, and wrote to her stepmother:

> Mr Cadogan is the real treasure; it certainly is unexpected and undeserved to have come all the way to Tehran and to find someone so delightful at the end . . . . He appears to have read everything that ought to be read in French, German and English.

Gertrude and Henry Cadogan were kindred spirits and their romance blossomed in the beauty of the Persian landscape. He contrived to join her on the numerous excursions she took into the Persian countryside, usually with auntie Mary and her cousin Florence, often with her new-found friends, the Rosens. Dr Rosen was the German chargé d'affaires in Tehran; his wife, Nina, had been a friend of Florence Bell's since the time she had lived in Paris.

On one such excursion Gertrude and Henry Cadogan

> lay under some trees in long grass . . . with a little stream at our feet, looking at the lights changing on the snow mountains and reading Catullus from a tiny volume which Mr Cadogan produced out of his pocket. It was very delicious.

In June the British Legation left the heat of Tehran and moved to the cooler hill-station of Gulahek. Gertrude wrote home of her idyllic life — the rich detail of her description takes us with her through meadows and up mountain tracks. Her writing was at its most lyrical:

> We rode up and up the gorge; at the bottom there were regiments of tall single hollyhocks growing by the side of the torrent, yellow, pink and red, and battalions of willows climbing up the rocky side; but these were left behind and still we went up through absolute desolation until after about an hour's climb we came out on to the top of the shoulder and suddenly worlds upon unknown worlds lay before us . . . . It was very wonderful in that great bare silence watching the shadows of the mountains creeping over the plain below, eating up first the green villages, then Tehran and at last the far hill beyond. As we came near Imam Zadeh, Mr Cadogan and I who were in front heard the Muezzin calling to prayer from the top of the shrine. It sounded very solemn, if one had only known which way Mecca lay one would like to have recited a little of the Koran oneself!

While Gertrude wrote to her stepmother of beauty and romance, her letters to her father were preoccupied with the latest political crisis in England. Salisbury's Conservative government was crumbling and in July there would be another general election. The Liberal Unionists who had split with Gladstone over Home Rule for Ireland were now a quite separate party and their new leader, Joseph Chamberlain, firmly rejected any future possibility of rejoining with the Liberals. The radical element of the Liberal party had launched a new programme of reform; called the 'Newcastle Programme', it included Irish Home Rule and local government reform. Gertrude's father was being pressed by the Unionists to stand for Parliament but he consistently refused. Then in July he sent a telegram to Gertrude. At the last minute he had decided to stand as a candidate for Middlesbrough. Six days later, after the election, a second telegram arrived from her father. Gertrude replied:

> I was very sorry to get your telegram though I did not expect you would have stood if you had thought it probable that you

would be returned. I am longing to hear the ins and outs of it all.

She soon learnt that Gladstone, then eighty-three years old, was Prime Minister for the fourth time, with a majority of forty over the opposition. But the Conservatives maintained the whip hand during the following few years of Liberal government. Soon after the election Gladstone submitted his Home Rule Bill; it was thrown out by the House of Lords where there was an overwhelming Unionist majority.

Gertrude had planned to stay in Persia for a year, but she was already homesick and wrote anxiously to her father asking him to come and bring her home in the autumn. She suggested they return by a route via Shiraz to

see the tomb of Khayyam and the palace of Darius and go straight on through the most . . . lovely country to Bushire. The very thought of it makes me wild to go, oh do say yes!'.

Her father sent a telegram on 24 July saying that he would come and collect her, returning via Shiraz. But within a few days of receiving the telegram all Gertrude's plans for the future were in flux. She had become engaged to Henry Cadogan:

I am in a panic lest you never received the letter I wrote to Mother on the 25th telling you that I was engaged to Mr Cadogan — if you have not this will come with rather a shock!

It was a shock. But the Bells reacted immediately — they refused to allow her to marry him. They maintained that Henry Cadogan had insufficient income to marry; but with Gertrude the daughter of a millionaire that would scarcely seem an obstacle. Although Gertrude was twenty-four, she accepted uncritically her father's ruling:

I do so long and long to be with you, the only drawback to it all is a horrible dread of having to say a quite indefinite goodbye to Mr Cadogan, for of course if Papa says it is quite all out of the question there will be nothing for him to do but to stay on in Persia for at least a year or more, perhaps two, and for us both nothing but to wait until he is Ambassador or something surprising and remunerative. The consolation is that people really do get on in this profession and make enough to live on before so very many years.

Before being escorted home in September, Gertrude went on a final excursion with the British Legation. It took them to the mountains north of Tehran: excursion is scarcely the right word for this venture, for they were retreating from the cholera that was sweeping through Persia. Gertrude's vivid description of the spread of the cholera appeared in a series of essays, *Safar Nameh. Persian Pictures*, published in 1894:

> In vain the desert was dotted over with the little white tents of fugitives, in vain they sought refuge in the cool mountain villages. Wherever they went they bore the plague in the midst of them; they dropped dead by the roadside, they died in the sand of the wilderness, they spread the fatal infection among the country people.

Although there had been major cholera epidemics throughout the nineteenth century, the epidemic of 1892 brought new horrors. The disease spread world wide with unprecedented rapidity. This was in striking contrast to all former epidemics and was attributed to the improvements that had been made in travel by railway and by steamboat. The march of the disease was traced day by day. It began in the North-West Provinces of India and in March 1892 was carried by Hindu pilgrims leaving the fair at Hardawar, on to Kabul in Afghanistan. By summer it was in Tehran; by early August in St Petersburg, then on to Hamburg; mid-August in Scotland and by the end of August it reached New York. The disease did not get a foothold in Britain or America; it was contained within the ships on which it arrived. But in Persia about 64,000 people died in the 1892 epidemic, and the mortality figure world wide was 380,000.

At the time Gertrude's letters home scarcely hinted at the horrors of the epidemic; she wrote mainly of details of her idyllic life camping near the banks of the River Lar, in the shadow of Demavend, the highest peak of the mountain range to the north of Tehran. It was Gertrude's first camping trip:

It has been rather an experience to realise the joy of it and the joy is great; I shall be sorry to leave this wonderful freedom and be back within walls and gardens.

It was a large camp: the Lascelles, the Rosens and other friends were there, and, of course, Mr Cadogan. Her life overbrimmed with romance:

> After tea we wandered down the stream Mr. Cadogan fishing. I talking to him and sitting down to read when he was on the opposite bank. It was the loveliest afternoon, sun and cloud on Demavend which gleamed brown and snow-white and grey, touches of sun on the valley and low creeping lines of soft cloud coming across the lowest hills. We came in very late, De-mavend flushed red and pink and faded into solemn cold grey and then came the dark and we walked home together talking.

She walked and climbed, fished and read, and swam 'in cold swift water'. A month later she left Persia. In her last letter home from Persia she wrote to her stepmother:

> The thing I can bear least is that you or Papa should ever think anything of him which is not noble and gentle and good . . . . Everything I think and write brings us back to things we have spoken together, sentences of his that come flashing like sharp swords; you see for the last three months nothing I have done or thought has not had him in it, the essence of it all.

A year later Henry Cadogan was dead. The story goes that he fell into those cold swift waters of the River Lar, waters where Gertrude swam just one year before. But Henry Cadogan died of a chill a few days later.

Gertrude's romance with Mr Cadogan was not a fleeting passion. It was not tempered by separation as her parents had hoped. Three-and-a-half years after she said her last farewell to him Gertrude, then in Venice, wrote in her diary:

> In a moment St. Mark's sprang up in front of us. I confess I felt very much inclined to cry. The band played, and the Piazzetta was full of people, and it seemed too silly, but the whole place was full of Henry Cadogan, and too lovely not to be sad.

Gertrude's stay in Persia and all her experiences there must have haunted her through her Persian studies for years after she left. Her translation of the *Poems from the Divan of Hafiz* was not completed and published until 1897. And in 1894 Richard Bentley published a collection of Gertrude's essays on Persia. Most of them were written while she was still in the country, the rest were composed on Bentley's request. The book *Safar Nameh. Persian Pictures. A book of travel* was published anonymously. Gertrude really did not want to see these essays in print. She wrote to her friend Flora Russell:

> Bentley wishes to publish my Persian things . . . I would vastly prefer them remain unpublished . . . . At first I refused, then my mother thought me mistaken and my father was disappointed and as they are generally right I have given way. But in my heart I hold very firmly to my first opinion. Don't speak of this. I wish them not to be read.

Safar Nameh, literally translated as 'Travelogue', received some good reviews when published but the book rarely has the vigour and atmosphere of her letters. But it does stand at a watershed in her life, for Persia was her first experience of the East, her first encounter with non-European culture. She felt new passions, not just for Henry Cadogan, but for Persia — its language, its culture, its desert beauty. She would be drawn to the East time and time again: as a traveller, an archaeologist and then officially in the diplomatic service. But all that lay hidden in the future, and after heady times in Persia she spent the next five years in the peaceful confines of upper-middle-class English society.

3 Emerging Alone

By the end of 1896 Gertrude had finished her translation of poems from the *Divan of Hafiz*. It was as if she had finally laid her Persian ghosts to rest. Certainly 1897 shows the first stirrings of new vigour in her life after five years spent almost entirely at home.

In January 1897 she joined the Lascelles family once again. Sir Frank had left Persia and, after a brief appointment in 1894 as British ambassador in Russia, became ambassador in Berlin. Gertrude was soon sharing with them the fun of European diplomatic social life, although she did note on 12 February that 'Uncle Frank is in a great jig about Crete. He thinks there is going to be red war and an intervention of the powers and all sorts of fine things'.

Gertrude's feelings of high excitement were not going to be dampened by the prospect of war. But uncle Frank had good grounds for anxiety — only two days later the Greeks landed on Crete to support the revolt of the Christians against their Turkish rulers. A Graeco-Turkish war was imminent, perhaps bringing a European war in its wake with Germany and Britain in direct conflict.

On the evening of 17 February the Lascelles family and Gertrude went to the theatre to see Shakespeare's *Henry IV*. In the interval they were invited to join Emperor William II and his empress in the royal box; during the customary tea-party Gertrude noticed:

A sheaf of telegrams were handed to the Emperor . . . . He and Uncle fell into an excited conversation in low voices; we talked to the Empress trying to pretend we heard nothing but catching scraps of the Emperor's remarks "Crete . . . Bulgaria . . . Servia . . . mobilizing" and so forth. The Empress kept looking at him anxiously — she is terribly perturbed about it all and no wonder for he is persuaded that we are all on the brink of war.

The telegrams the emperor had just received no doubt gave

details of the latest developments on Crete. Within the preceding forty-eight hours an armed contingent had been sent by the Powers (Britain, France, Italy, Russia, Austria and Germany) to immobilize the occupying Greek force. Although it had succeeded in its mission the troubles were far from over. There were Greeks determined to trigger war with Turkey, hoping to win Macedonia as a prize in such a conflict. And each country in Europe was poised to snatch parts of the Ottoman Empire whenever it would finally disintegrate.

Turkey was highly vulnerable and would never be able to withstand an attack from an efficient European army and its technically advanced armaments. But Britain was one of the countries that sought to preserve this decadent, unstable Empire, recognizing the scramble for territory that would follow its collapse.

The European powers acted in concert this time although there was growing discord between Germany and the rest of Europe. At the theatre tea-party Gertrude witnessed the close friendship that existed between Sir Frank and the emperor despite the increasing estrangement of their two nations.

Within a year Germany and Austria left the united European Powers to ally themselves politically with Turkey. But a major war was averted. Crete was given autonomy and the Ottoman empire otherwise remained intact. It was the final dismemberment of the Ottoman empire, following the First World War, that gave Gertrude the opportunity to exercise power and influence in the British diplomatic service. But those years were still a long way off. In 1897 she could still enjoy the social whirl of diplomatic life: skating and sledging parties, dinners and dances. But she did admit to tedium when faced with the prospect of a third court ball and appealed to her father to let her return home.

Later that year the whole Bell family went on holiday to La Grave in Dauphiné, the Alpine region of south-east France. Gertrude had her first experience of mountain climbing. Nothing very demanding but just enough to make her determined to return and climb the Meije. At 13,081 feet it is the second highest peak in the Dauphiné Alps, and had been first climbed just twenty years earlier. Most of the more challenging Alpine peaks had been conquered in the 1860s or 1870s. Since the middle of the century mountain climbing had become a sport: the techniques of

Gertrude Bell.

climbing had been perfected; there was a body of professional guides; the Alpine Club was founded (first in Britain in 1857 then in other European countries) and its members systematically climbed the Alps. But it was of course very unusual to find a woman reaching the highest peaks; and it was the highest peaks that Gertrude climbed during the next six years.

But first — a six-months Cook's tour of the world, leaving Southampton in December 1897, accompanied by brother Maurice. 'It is not worth while reproducing all that she and Maurice saw on this well-known route', wrote Florence Bell when editing the letters of her stepdaughter. Indeed the route had been traversed by the wealthy since 1873 when Thomas Cook himself conducted the first world tour. In the 1890s the six-month tour cost about £450 per person; but Sir Hugh would have had to pay even more for the detours that were included in Gertrude's and Maurice's itinerary, such as visits to Guatemala and Jamaica.

In August 1899 Gertrude was back in the Dauphiné Alps and on the 28th a telegram was on its way to Yorkshire — 'Meije traversée'. In a letter to her father she wrote:

> I think if I had known exactly what was before me I should not have faced it, but fortunately I did not, and I look back on it with unmixed satisfaction — and forward to other things with no further apprehension.

Gertrude's new-found courage would soon lead her to the lonely, wild deserts of the Middle East. Just three months after her conquest of the Meije she was heading east to Jerusalem at the invitation of the Rosens. They had become 'great friends' when Gertrude met them in Persia. Dr Rosen was now the German consul-general in Jerusalem and Gertrude's visit had no doubt been anticipated for some years. She had certainly begun learning Arabic in England for two or three years and was able to read the *Arabian Nights* in the original. But when she arrived in Jerusalem Gertrude found that conversation presented considerable problems:

> I am just beginning to understand a little of what I hear and to say simple things to servants, but I find it awfully difficult. The pronunciation is past words, no western throat being constructed to form these extraordinary gutturals . . . I don't think I shall ever talk Arabic, but I go on struggling with it in the hope of mortifying Providence by my persistence. I now stammer a few words to my housemaid — him of the fez — and he is much delighted.

25

Gertrude soon began Arabic lessons and in later life was a renowned Arab linguist with a remarkable ear for the subtleties of dialect!

Gertrude's stay in Jerusalem was a joy to her from the first. She soon began to explore the city and its immediate environs, and as always wrote home long descriptive letters of all she saw. But on 5 January 1900 her letter to her stepmother began: 'What a terrible time it is. I feel such a beast writing to you about my pleasant doings in the midst of all this.'

Gertrude must recently have heard the news of 'black week', a week in late December 1899 when the British suffered heavy casualties in the war they were fighting against the Boers in the Transvaal in South Africa. The British army was depleted of trained soldiers; the responsibility for the British defence would fall to a volunteer force mustered back in Britain. It was inevitable that Gertrude's brother Maurice would be among their number. It was only a matter of time before he would join the carnage in South Africa.

The Boers had considerable strength in the field and had been importing German arms in preparation for war for more than a year. They had laid siege to three British strongholds: Kimberley, Ladysmith and Mafeking. They were determined to oust the British force from South Africa and perpetuate the virtual dictatorship set up by Kruger.

In December 1899 the Boers, with more than 40,000 men in the field, greatly outnumbered the British army but before the end of the next year the commander of the British forces, Lord Kitchener, had over 200,000 soldiers under his command, all volunteers, stirred by an awesome rise in nationalism in Britain. Maurice went out in February 1900, an officer in the Volunteer Service Company of the Yorkshire Regiment.

Gertrude wrote home in February from Jerusalem: 'It is rather terrible to think that Maurice is off. I hoped he wouldn't leave to the end of the month'. There was a firm belief among the British that the volunteer reinforcements would quickly relieve the three British strongholds under siege, and the war would draw to a swift close.

On 2 March Gertrude wrote to her stepmother: 'Today came the joyful news of the relief of Ladysmith'. Her letter continued with details of the expeditions she planned. Within three weeks

Gertrude had set off on the first of her desert journeys. Complete with mules, muleteers, Bedouin guide and soldier escort, she went into Moab, a desert region east of the Dead Sea. Within two days she was at the ruins of the Persian Palace at Mashetta. She described the visit:

> The beauty of it all was quite past words. It's a thing one will never forget as long as one lives. At last, most reluctantly, we turned back on our four hours' ride home. We hadn't gone more than a few yards before three of the Beni Sakhr came riding towards us, armed to the teeth, black browed and most menacing. When they saw our soldier, they threw us the salaam with some disgust and . . . proceeded on their way — we felt that the interview might have turned out differently if we had been unescorted.

All travellers through this part of the Ottoman empire were required by the Turkish authorities to have a soldier escort and the local governor's permission. Gertrude did not always travel with either.

Two days later Gertrude was planning to travel south to Petra, a journey of about fifty miles. She had got the necessary permission and a soldier escort but only by pretending to be German — 'for they are desperately afraid of the English', Gertrude wrote home. The Turks were very suspicious of the British, believing that they intended to annex parts of the Ottoman empire in the Middle East. To the Turks every British traveller venturing into the desert regions was probably a spy, trying to establish allies among the disparate Arab tribes, perhaps even organizing an Arab uprising. The soldier escort was provided ostensibly only to protect the traveller from marauding Arab tribesmen, but the authorities insisted on an escort even on trips where there was little hazard.

Gertrude found it an irresistible challenge to outwit the Turkish authorities and in early May she contrived a plan to misinform Turkish officials of her intended route so that she might embark on a journey into the heart of the Druze country. The Turks feared the Druze and certainly did not want the British to have any contact with them, but Gertrude evaded the Turkish authorities. She was camped outside the town walls of Bosrah and sneaked off in the middle of the night. She

> prayed Heaven that no soldier would look over the castle wall,
> see our lantern, and come to enquire what was happening. . . .
> At 4 we were off. It was a ticklish business finding our way in
> the dark round the walls. . . . It took us near an hour. . . .
> Muhammud [one of her servants] was trembling lest he should
> see either a Druze or a soldier. I feared the latter only, but
> much.

She was soon enjoying the protection and hospitality of the
Druze. She travelled through the Druze country and then returned to Damascus. She was already buzzing with plans for her
next journey — to Palmyra, the ancient ruined city in the middle
of the Syrian desert.

> Dearest father! you are a perfect angel to let me do all this! I
> don't see that the Palmyra journey ought to be much more
> expensive than all the others. It seems I shan't have to take
> more than three soldiers at the outside. . . . It is at times a very
> odd sensation to be out in the world quite by myself.

It was a long, tiring desert journey to Palmyra, and Gertrude's
caravan moved slowly from water-hole to water-hole. At one
watering place 'the water was clear and cold but . . . full of
swimming things of all kinds . . . I shut my eyes and drank'. But
Gertrude never complained of the physical hardships and depri-
vations of desert travel. She was in her element and wrote to her
father: 'One doesn't keep away from the East when one has got
into it this far'.

The visit to Palmyra was complete joy: 'except Petra, Palmyra
is the loveliest thing I have seen in this country'. And on her
return to Damascus she found 'Telegrams from you and the war
news excellent'. The news must have been of Britain's annexation
a few days before of the Orange Free State in South Africa. The
British must have felt that the war's end was in sight but the
Boers continued a bitter guerilla war; peace did not come for a
further two years.

Gertrude was in high spirits when she left the Middle East in
the early June of 1900. But as always her longing for home began
to overshadow her excitement at visiting new places. She wrote to

her father: 'We shall go to Jaffa to-morrow, as there is a boat and I am anxious to get home. But you know, dearest Father, I shall be back here before long.'

Before returning to the Middle East she had other things she was determined to achieve. The peaks of the Alps were beckoning her.

She spent either July or August of 1901, 1902 and 1903 climbing in the Alps. These are the best months for climbing and during those years she climbed the Finsteraarhorn (14,026 feet), the highest peak in the Bernese Oberland, and was the first to explore systematically the peaks of the Engelhorner group, making several first ascents. One of the newly-conquered peaks was given the name 'Gertrude's Peak', another was named after one of her guides, Ulrich Fuhrer.

Gertrude's letters home captured the risk and thrill of mountain climbing. On 3 August 1902 she wrote to her father of her assault on Finsteraarhorn. She had with her two experienced guides, the brothers Ulrich and Heinrich Fuhrer. It was probably her most testing climbing venture; the descent was treacherous:

> I had a pain through my shoulder and down my back which was due, I think, to nothing but the exertion of rock climbing and the nervous fatigue of shivering — for we never stopped shivering all day. . . . We tried to make a tent out of my skirt and to light a match under it, but our fingers were dripping wet and numb with cold . . . and the match heads dropped off limply into the snow without so much as a spark. Then we tried to go on and after a few steps Heinrich fell into a soft place almost up to his neck and Ulrich and I had to pull him out with the greatest difficulty and the mists swept over the glacier and hid everything.

After this climb she suffered severe frost-bite in her toes and fingers, but her spirit was irrepressible and two years later she would be back up in the Alps again with the two Fuhrer brothers. But a few months after the Finsteraarhorn adventure she set off on another six-month world tour, this time with her stepbrother, Hugo.

Their route took them directly to India, arriving in time for the Delhi durbar which began on New Year's Eve. At this magnificent ceremonial gathering the coronation of the new king was proclaimed: Edward VII, King of the United Kingdom of Great Britain and Ireland, and all the British Dominions beyond the seas; defender of the faith; Emperor of India. Edward was not present at the durbar because he was still recovering from an appendicitis operation he had had in June. But he had previously visited India in 1876 preparing the way for the declaration in 1877 of Queen Victoria as Empress of India, which had also been celebrated with a durbar.

The durbar of 1903 was an immensely impressive spectacle. The preparations had taken months and were supervised by the viceroy himself, Lord Curzon. The cost was immense and the source of much criticism in Britain and India. But for Curzon this occasion marked the summit of the viceregal splendour he so relished. It was an event on the calendar of London society, and Gertrude found herself among a host of friends, relatives, acquaintances; on the Delhi polo ground she 'met all the world'.

From Delhi she visited other cities in north India and then moved east round the world, leaving India far behind, little realizing that one day she would return — an important guest of the viceroy himself.

She returned to England from the world tour in July 1903; obviously there was not time to go climbing in the Alps before the end of the season. Her next climb came the following August, when she scaled the Matterhorn accompanied, as always, by the Fuhrer brothers. It was her last climb. From now on, the challenge came from the East and she spent most of her travels of the next ten years in the deserts of the Middle East and in remote parts of Asia Minor. She was now ready to be out in the world quite alone.

4 Adventure and Archaeology

While her sisters were marrying, producing children, and passing their days chatting over tea in the drawing-rooms of polite society, Gertrude took her caravan of mules, camels and servants into the desert; visiting great sheikhs; sipping coffee; 'deep in the gossip of the East'.

It was 1905 when she undertook her first serious expedition into the desert. She recorded her travels in her book *Syria: The Desert and the Sown*, published two years later. Here she graphically described the challenge such a journey presented:

> The world of adventure and of enterprise, dark with hurrying storms, glittering in raw sunlight, an unanswered question and unanswerable doubt hidden in the fold of every hill. Into it you must go alone. . .roofless, defenceless, without possessions. The voice of the wind shall be heard instead of the persuasive voices of counsellors, the touch of the rain and the prick of the frost shall be spurs sharper than praise or blame.

On this journey she ventured into parts of the Syrian desert where she was the first European woman ever to have been seen. The sheikhs always treated her as they would any distinguished male guest. Sometimes Gertrude was taken to the harem to visit the women, but she ate and talked with the men. And she of course made it clear that she came from 'a great and honoured stock', and expected to be treated as her rank deserved.

Gertrude could enjoy the prestige of being English at a time when Britain was boldly asserting influence and authority in the East. On 27 February 1905 she wrote home from Damascus:

> I believe the fact of my being English is a great help . . . . We have gone up in the world since five years ago. The difference is very marked. I think it is due to the success of our government in Egypt to a great extent . . . . The defeat of Russia stands for a great deal, and my impression is that the vigorous policy of Lord Curzon in the Persian Gulf and on the Indian frontier stands for a great deal more. No one who does not know the

East can realise how closely it all hangs together. It is scarcely an exaggeration to say that if the English mission had been turned back from the gates of Kabul, the English tourist would be frowned upon in the streets of Damascus.

It was essential for Britain to maintain a position of authority in the Middle East. It was here that lay the land and sea routes from the Mediterranean to India. Much of British foreign policy at this time was directed towards ensuring the security of these routes and the security of the frontiers of India itself.

Lord Curzon, viceroy of India, had insisted on a policy that gave Britain the upper hand throughout the Persian Gulf. The Turks wanted a harbour on the Gulf, in Kuwait. Curzon authorized Kuwait to be placed under British protection. He also paid a state visit to the Gulf in November 1903. It was — in the style of Lord Curzon — a spectacular display of British naval supremacy and it was obvious that British predominance in the Gulf could not be challenged. Furthermore announcements from London made it clear to the Russians that the British would not tolerate any plans they had for moving into southern Persia in order to gain a port on the Gulf.

Gertrude's February letter also refers to two other recent developments in world events which gave Britain the upper hand over Russia and increased prestige among the Arabs. While Gertrude was writing her letter in Damascus, Curzon's diplomatic mission in Kabul was concluding a treaty with Afghanistan. That treaty, signed in March 1905, strengthened relations between Afghanistan and India and prevented any Russian encroachment.

Gertrude's 1905 visit to the Middle East also coincided with a series of humiliating defeats for Russia in the Russo-Japanese War. The war had begun a year earlier in February 1904 and was now drawing to a close. The British had supported the Japanese throughout this war.

The fighting had taken place in China where Russia had, since 1900, slowly extended its sphere of influence southwards through Manchuria. But the Japanese drove the Russian army back into northern Manchuria. This conquest by an oriental nation of a mighty western power had a tremendous impact among the oppressed peoples of the Ottoman empire. And of course Britain emerged as the champion of the eastern underdog.

When Gertrude writes of the 'East' or the 'Orient' she was using terms which earlier this century included the area we now refer to as the Middle East. At this time Britain had a clear policy towards all 'Eastern' peoples: they needed to be integrated into the modern world; they needed to be supervised and reorganized along western lines — in short, they needed the British. It was 'divine Providence' that had ordained that the British should direct and develop the peoples of India — that was Lord Curzon's fervent belief. Even if this was an extreme view, Britain felt a responsibility to exercise authority over the disordered societies of the East. Gertrude wrote in the preface of her book *The Desert and the Sown*: 'Being English I am persuaded that we are the people who could best have taken Syria in hand.' The book is dedicated to 'A.C.L.', her friend Sir Alfred Comyn Lyall, 'who knows the heart of the east'. He was a British administrator in India with strong views on British practice when ruling foreign peoples: these so-called 'Lyallist doctrines' insisted that the British show respect for the institutions and traditional beliefs of the native people, and that British rule was conducted through local institutions and the native ruling class. Egypt was held to be the perfect example.

The British and French had exercised 'dual control' in Egypt since 1882 with the intention of sorting out Egypt's considerable financial problems and, of course, ensuring the secure passage of their shipping through the Suez Canal. But since 1883 it was the British who effectively ruled Egypt. The British agent Lord Cromer, uncle of Gertrude's friend Maurice Baring, did ostensibly act as an adviser to Egyptian ministers but he was an autocrat who insisted that Egyptian ministers and governors followed his advice or forfeited their posts.

There was considerable pride among the British for Cromer's rule in Egypt. There were remarkable improvements in the country's financial status, and the introduction of perennial irrigation dramatically boosted agricultural yields. But there were many frustrated, educated and able Egyptians who resented what they saw as British oppression. They joined societies and political parties which were nationalistic and anti-British.

But for the Arab in the Syrian desert Gertrude found that 'Egypt is a sort of promised land, you have no idea what an impression our government there has made on the Oriental mind.' She wrote in her book *The Desert and the Sown*:

All over Syria and even in the desert, whenever a man is ground down by injustice or mastered by his own incompetence, he wishes that he were under the rule that has given wealth to Egypt, and our occupation of that country, which did so much at first to alienate from us the sympathy of Mohammedans, has proved the finest advertisement of English methods of government.

Gertrude herself saw Egypt as an unmitigated British success. She could hardly have been unaware of the surge of nationalistic feeling in Egypt, but she was, as all the British were, unimpressed and unconcerned. Her views would change after the First World War and she would become an outspoken and authoritative supporter of self-rule for Arab nations. In 1905, however, it was unthinkable for the British that eastern peoples could progress without a long-term British presence to supervise them.

And so Gertrude ventured into the Syrian desert in February 1905, a supremely confident member of the British upper-middle class — born and bred to command respect wherever she travelled.

Her travels began with a short stay in Jerusalem where she consulted Mark Sykes, a famous desert traveller, who was also planning a trip into the Syrian desert. She comments after visiting him and his wife Edith: 'They received me with open arms, kept me to dinner and we spent the merriest of evenings. They are perfectly charming.' Within a few days Mark Sykes was recording his opinion of Gertrude as he set off into the desert; he was convinced that she was an 'infernal liar' and had taken 'the very route I told her I hoped to do, after she said she was going elsewhere'. And he wished '10,000 of my worst bad words on the head of that damned fool' when, through Gertrude's indiscretion, he was unable to get the necessary Turkish permission to continue his travels from Damascus. Gertrude had, it seemed, idly told the Kaimakam of Salk that Mark's brother-in-law was prime minister of Egypt, when in fact he was a financial adviser to the Khedive. Mark Sykes did not ascribe malicious motives to Gertrude but wrote to his wife describing her as a 'silly chattering windbag of conceited, gushing, flat-chested, man-woman, globe-trotting, rump-wagging, blethering *ass*'.

Gertrude had certainly left Jerusalem very promptly and no doubt intended to keep ahead of Mark Sykes during her desert travels. On the first stage of her journey she camped by the Jordan Bridge where 'there passed through this morning 900 soldiers on their way to help Ibn Rashid in Central Arabia'. This was one of two columns the Turks sent to help restore their protégé Ibn Rashid to his capital Ha'il, which had been threatened by Ibn Saud. By the beginning of March the Turks were camped near Ha'il but then withdrew their troops, having decided not to embark on a full-scale campaign in the Nejd (central Arabia). Instead the whole matter was settled by gifts from the Sultan to both parties; peace was made and the Rashids safely installed in Ha'il.

The outcome seems to have been a foregone conclusion among the peoples of the desert, for in early February Gertrude was already planning with her friend Namoud 'an immense journey for the winter after next, no less than to Ibn Rashid' — a journey to Ha'il itself. Namoud was not planning in ignorance for he knew 'every sheikh of all the Bedouin for miles and miles around'.

Wherever Gertrude travelled in the desert she 'laid the foundations of friendship with several important people — of desert importance that is', thereby helping to ensure safe passage on any future trips. Her method of securing Arab friendship belonged more to the drawing-room than the desert. She wrote of a meeting with a great sheikh, Humeidi Beg Ibn Farhan: 'I gave him my visiting card and he bade me welcome to all the Shammar tents'. So Gertrude extended her circle of important, influential friends to include the sheikhs of the desert.

Whether in London or in the Middle East Gertrude thrived on being the centre of attention. And, of course, wherever she travelled she did excite interest; even on her first visit in 1902 she wrote from Mount Carmel:

I am much entertained to find that I am a person in this country . . . and one of the first questions everyone seems to ask everyone else is "Have you ever met Miss Gertrude Bell?" Renown is not very difficult to acquire here.

She recorded the sort of reception she enjoyed in the desert in 1905:

> I am the first woman who has ever been in these parts . . . . I established myself on the divan, all the Druzes sitting round in rows and answered all their questions about foreign parts, especially Japan for they are thrilled over the war.

And then in Damascus:

> I find the Government here was in an agony of nervousness all the time I was in the Jebel Druze! They had three telegrams a day from Salkhad about me. . .I have become a Person in Syria! . . . Every afternoon I hold a reception and Damascus flocks to drink my coffee and converse with me.

Within two years she really became a celebrated traveller and was fêted at home and abroad. In 1907 when she arrived in Constantinople after archaeological excavations in Asia Minor she was immediately taken to see the Grand Vizier and then spent her days receiving a stream of visits from 'troops of professors and people of that kind', which was of course 'vastly entertaining'. Her return to London some days later found her in celebrated British company:

> Today I lunched with Sir Edward and Mr Haldane — Willie told Sir E I was here and he quickly asked me to lunch. Sir Frank is coming to tea and I dine with Domnul and spend the balance of the evening, after he goes to the office with Willie T. Sir Henry C B hasn't sent for me yet — I'm a little surprised aren't you?

Quite a line up! Sir Edward Grey, the Foreign Secretary; Willie Tyrell, Sir Edward's highly influential Principal Private Secretary; Mr Haldane, Secretary of State for War; Sir Frank Swettenham, recently retired High Commissioner for the Malay States; Domnul, Gertrude's close and influential friend; Sir Henry Campbell-Bannerman, Prime Minister.

Did Gertrude venture into the desert merely to be outrageous and gain notoriety? Surely not. There seem to be two reasons why

Caricature of Gertrude Bell

the desert attracted her so strongly — the adventure and the possibility of archaeological discovery.

She relished the risk and adventure; and when desert trekking became monotonous she yearned 'that something would happen — something exciting, a raid or a battle!', and she regretted whenever she missed a *ghazu* — a raid. You can sense the thrill she felt when in her travels of 1900 she outwitted the Turkish authorities and crept away under the cover of dark from the town of Bosrah. And on the 1905 expedition into the Syrian desert she wrote:

> I laugh to think I am marching along the Turkish frontier, so to speak, some ten miles beyond it, and they can't catch me or stop me. It is rather fun to have outwitted them a second time.

It was a game — a game often with high stakes, for her life was at risk; though that risk was probably much less for her than for a

male European traveller, as it would have brought shame on a
Bedouin to kill a lone woman. However, she did run the constant
risk of a raiding party taking all her possessions and leaving her
without supplies.

But the adventure alone did not provide sufficient intellectual
fulfilment for Gertrude's prodigious intelligence. The adventure
was secondary; it was her archaeological studies that kept her
moving through the desert and on to remoter parts of Asia Minor.

On the 1905 expedition she went through northern Syria into
Asia Minor to study the early Byzantine churches. Her travels
ended at Binbirklisse, the place of a thousand and one churches
— a name given not to describe the exact number of churches but
the Turkish way of indicating a large unspecified number. It was
an area that was attracting a considerable amount of archaeological interest. She wrote to her father excitedly as soon as she
arrived:

> If you had (and who knows? Perhaps you have!) the very latest
> German archaeology books you would be wild with excitement
> at seeing where I am.

And she continued with a description of the region:

> Binbirklisse. . .lies at the foot of the Kara Dagh, a great iso-
> lated mountain arising abruptly out of the plain and . . . it
> must have been a very important early Christian city for it is
> full of churches dating back Strzygowski thinks to pre-
> Constantine times. There is a lower town down at the foot of
> the hills and an upper town about an hour from it on a
> shoulder of mountain, and fate and my zaptieh ordered by
> good luck that our road should lead us to the upper town first. I
> fell in love with it at once, a mass of beautiful ruins gathered
> together in a little rocky cup high up in the hills — with Asia
> Minor at its feet.

Gertrude stayed high up in the Kara Dagh for several days
making plans of the church ruins she found there and soon
published her results in a letter to the *Revue Archéologique*. The site
had not only attracted the attention of the foremost German
archaeologist Josef Strzygowski but also that of the leading
British epigraphist and archaeologist Sir William Ramsay. He

also was visiting Binbirklisse at the same time as Gertrude and they met up at Konia. Gertrude showed him an inscription from one of the churches which she believed contained a date. Ramsay wrote later:

> Her belief proved well founded, and the chronology of the Thousand and One Churches centres round this text. . .I printed in the *Athenaeum* the impression made on me by a hurried inspection of the ruins, mainly in order to reiterate in more precise form my old hope that an important architectural and historical investigation might be performed by an architect and epigraphist, combining their work for a month or two on the site. This letter attracted her attention; she wrote suggesting that we should undertake the task; and as no one else seemed likely to do so, my wife and I arranged to join her in 1907.

Ramsay does not write of Gertrude's offer of cooperation with much enthusiasm. Accomplished, aspiring young archaeologists competed to work with Ramsay — but Gertrude's offer had other attractions, she insisted on paying for all the expedition expenses and she had shown a good eye for important detail when uncovering the date inscription.

In May 1907 the Ramsays arrived at Maden Sheher, the lower town at the foot of the Kara Dagh. Gertrude was waiting for them and had made complete preparations for their arrival, which was just as well since the Ramsays travelled chaotically and totally unprepared for anything. Gertrude records that Captain Doughty-Wylie, now vice-consul at Konia, wrote to her of the Ramsays' arrival at Konia entirely without tents or possessions. He continued:

> Nevertheless Ramsay was most eager to set off to join you at once — in the wrong direction. I lent him two tents and headed him off towards you.

Gertrude and Sir William worked in the region of Binbirklisse for just four weeks collecting a mass of material which they planned to turn into a book: 'Sir W shall write the historic and epigraphic part and I the architectural'. Gertrude also noted that:

This is the very first time anyone has set about to explore thoroughly a single district in central Asia Minor. See what we have got out of it! Two great Hittite sites and a vast amount of unexpected Byzantine remains.

Although most of the work centred on the Byzantine ruins, there were unexpected Hittite finds. While digging at Kara Dagh Gertrude found a 'queer inscription' which Ramsay identified as Hittite. The inscription caused a considerable amount of interest and was published in the *Proceedings of the Society for Biblical Archaeology* by A.H. Sayce, professor of Assyriology at Oxford. At this time the script could not be translated but Sayce's powerful writings fired the imagination of archaeologists and Gertrude wrote a month later to her father: 'The learned world is agog about my Hittite inscription'. But from late 1907 onwards the real excitement came when the true history of the Hittites became known through the important discoveries of Hugo Winckler at Boghazkoy, where he found the Hittite royal archive. It is intriguing that even today Kara Dagh retains its secrets: we do know that the Hittite sites discovered by Gertrude and Sir William were set up by a ruler called Haraptus, but who he was or when he ruled remain a mystery!

Throughout 1908 she stayed at home writing *The Thousand and One Churches* in collaboration with Sir William Ramsay. It was published in 1909 and hailed as a classic of early Byzantine studies.

Despite her obvious enthusiasm when working with Ramsay in Asia Minor she had grave misgivings of her ability to continue any long-term work there as an archaeologist. She wrote to Domnul at the time:

This is not my country — I must break the fact gently to the good Ramsay. I have not the training for it; it demands the devotion of a lifetime, and that I cannot give — or will not . . . I shall go back to Arabia, to the desert where I can do things and see things that Ramsay and his learned like could scarcely do and see because they have not time enough or money enough for such enterprises. O bir safar! that's where it must take me.

From then on Gertrude's travels took her to the deserts of the

East, and wherever she ventured she sought new sites of archaeological interest — always hoping to find a hitherto undiscovered
treasure. During her desert journey of 1911 she wrote:

> As we rode across the desert he [her guide] said: "Do you want
> to go to Rakban?" "What is Rakban?" said I. "It is a castle of
> the first time" said he. . . . In a flash my mind ran out to the
> Lakhmid castles, which none of us had been able to trace. . . .
> Through a sandstorm then five hours from Musella we reached
> some waterpools, bitter salt but the horses drank there. An
> hour further. . .presently the black mass of the castle appeared
> in front of us. I plunged through the sand, reached it — and
> found it to be nothing but a mud-built enclosure, not 50 years
> old. . . . But what was I to do? I could not leave a ruin
> unvisited.

Just two years earlier in 1909 the same stretch of desert did
yield one of its treasures — an ancient castle. Gertrude was
camped on the edge of the desert to the west of the Euphrates.
She questioned the Arabs who had gathered round her camp-fire
about the north-west corner of the Sassanian empire. One of the
Arabs offered to take Gertrude to the castles there: 'Khubbâz,
'Amej, Themail and Kheidir'. Her ears pricked up at the name
Kheidir for she had never heard of it; when she tried to find out
more 'the sum total of the information offered by them seemed to
be that water was scarce and raids frequent, but there were
certainly castles'.

To reach Kheidir Gertrude travelled through the dangerous
tribal territory of the Duleim. On 26 March 1909 she arrived and
wrote exhuberantly:

> It is an enormous castle, fortress, palace — what you will, 155
> metres by 170 metres. . .the most undreamt of example of the
> finest Sassanian art that ever was. It is not seen on the map, it
> has never been published, I never heard its name before. . . .
> As soon as I saw it I decided that this was the opportunity of a
> lifetime.

In her first enthusiasm she became convinced that she had
found a palace of the Lakhmid princes:

The Arab historians relate that when the Mohammedans first conquered this country, in the seventh century, they stood in amazement before the Lakhmid palaces; as far as I know this is the only one that remains, and it is almost perfect.

She subsequently changed her opinion on the period of Ukhaidir's construction and when writing her book dated it as mid-eighth century — the palaces of the Lakhmid princes remained to be discovered. Her first publication on the palace of Ukhaidir was an article on the vaulting system published in the *Journal of Hellenic Studies* in 1910. A more detailed account of the building was given the following year in her book *Amurath to Amurath*. In 1911 she returned to Ukhaidir to check her plans and take additional measurements. In 1914 *Palace and Mosque at Ukhaidir* was published. But by this time Ukhaidir had generated considerable interest among archaeologists and a team of Germans had done a very thorough survey of the buildings. They published a book on Ukhaidir in 1912 and allowed Gertrude to use many of their architectural drawings in her own book.

Gertrude's books on archaeology were well received and her work was recognized for its thoroughness. She could easily have made archaeology her sole preoccupation for the rest of her life but she did not have the temperament to confine herself to academic pursuits. She had grown up in an atmosphere of strong political consciousness and when the opportunity came for her to exercise political influence it was irresistible. The debate on woman suffrage gave Gertrude her first chance of political involvement but soon she would be wielding her influence in middle-eastern politics.

Archaeology would always remain a profound interest of Gertrude's but for her, it was politics that gave life its spice.

_____

Gertrude Bell outside her tent at Babylon, 1909.

5 Woman's Position

At first sight Gertrude Bell seems an unconventional woman, perhaps even a pioneering feminist. So it might come as a surprise to find her in 1908 a founder-member of the Women's National Anti-Suffrage League, vigorously opposing the woman's right-to-vote campaign. But further investigation shows the anti-suffrage movement as a natural home for Gertrude.

The issue of woman suffrage had intermittently entered the political arena since 1867, when John Stuart Mill first put a woman suffrage bill before Parliament. It was heavily defeated. Over the next forty years Members of Parliament voted no less than eighteen times on the subject. On five occasions the supporters of woman suffrage gained a majority in the House of Commons, but their success amounted to no more than a declaration of principle — no Cabinet, Liberal or Conservative, would make woman suffrage a government measure.

The first clear statement of the anti-suffrage creed was published in 1889. The anti-suffragists rallied at this time because they felt that the Conservative government might support a bill giving the franchise to propertied spinsters and widows in the belief that these women would vote Conservative.

'An Appeal Against Female Suffrage' was published in June 1889 in *The Nineteenth Century*. It was written by Mrs Humphry Ward, long-time friend of the Bell family and champion of women's higher education in the University of Oxford. The 'Appeal' put its case bluntly:

> We believe that the emancipating process has now reached the limits fixed by the physical constitution of women, and by the fundamental difference which must always exist between their main occupations and those of men.

Indeed many reforms had been introduced in respect of women's civic role: in 1834 women were granted the right to vote for the Boards of Guardians who administered the Poor Law; in 1869 they were given the municipal vote and a year later the power to elect and be elected to school boards; in 1888 women were given the vote for the new county councils.

The 'Appeal' welcomed these changes but argued that:

> when it comes to questions of foreign or colonial policy, or grave constitutional change, then we maintain that the necessary and normal experience of women. . .does not and can never provide them with such materials for sound judgment as are open to men.

Astonishingly, these were the views that Gertrude Bell championed twenty years later when the anti-suffragists set up their first national organization. But already in 1889 she was surrounded by supporters of anti-suffrage.

The 'Appeal' was published with a list of the names of 104 prominent women who gave support. Heading the list was the Dowager Lady Stanley of Alderley, mother of Lyulph Stanley, who was married to Maisie, Hugh Bell's sister. Lady Stanley was a champion of women's higher education and especially had lent support to the foundation of Girton in Cambridge; indeed Gertrude's first inclination was to go to Girton and she was much embarrassed to inform Lady Stanley of her place at Lady Margaret Hall. The 1889 list interestingly contains other supporters of women's higher education — notably Mrs Humphry Ward herself, Mrs T.H. Green and Mrs Arnold Toynbee. All three were wives of Oxford dons who had been key figures in the setting up of Lady Margaret Hall — which Gertrude had left just three years before the 'Appeal'. Elizabeth Wordsworth, the Principal of LMH and a close friend of Mrs Toynbee, was also against woman suffrage although she never publicly gave her name to the cause.

Other names that appeared on the list of 104 included: Mrs J.R. Green, Mrs Poynter and Beatrice Potter (soon to be married to Sidney Webb) — all close friends of the Bell family. There were also the names of Mrs Matthew Arnold (Mrs Humphry Ward's aunt by marriage) and Mrs W.E. Forster (Matthew Arnold's sister). The list begins to emerge as a social fraternity — a fraternity in which the Bells were closely meshed.

In the July issue of *The Nineteenth Century*, the suffragist leader Mrs Fawcett replied to the 'Appeal' and drew attention to the fact that many on the list were peeresses and those 'to whom the lines of life have fallen in pleasant places'. Her article on the rights of woman suffrage was accompanied by another pro-suffrage statement, written by Mrs Dilke. It pointed out that the anti-suffrage movement was led by a group of women prominent in London society. Gertrude was very much at home in that circle.

In the August issue of *The Nineteenth Century* appeared a list of more than two thousand women who had signed the petition which appeared along with the 'Appeal' two months earlier. The petition read:

The undersigned protest strongly against the proposed Extension of the Parliamentary Franchise to Women which they believe would be a measure distasteful to the great majority of the women of the country — unnecessary — and mischievious both to themselves and to the state.

Many of the signatories belonged to the same social set as the initial 104. And although the signatories to both lists only consisted of women, there was strong anti-suffrage support among the prominent men of the time. Many of them acknowledged the political influence which the women of London society wielded. Indeed this was part of the Anti's creed: women with talent were already able to exercise considerable political influence; those unable to exercise such influence could not possibly be properly qualified to vote sensibly. Able women could achieve a great deal — they did not need the vote. Gertrude Bell became a shining example.

The 'Appeal' of 1889 failed to produce any organized anti-suffrage movement although there remained considerable activity in Parliament among Anti MPs. And so the issue of woman suffrage quietly simmered through the last years of the nineteenth century.

In 1903 a new suffragist organization, the Women's Social and Political Union, was founded by Mrs Pankhurst. It employed violent methods of protest and its militant members became known as 'suffragettes' — to distinguish them from the 'suffragists' of the old National Union. There had been great annoyance among suffragists at the political manoeuvrings which cheated them of the franchise; they were especially frustrated by the introduction of the subject of universal suffrage whenever they seemed near gaining some measure of female suffrage. This was seen as a device for shelving completely the question of woman suffrage, for Parliament showed great resistance to allowing a universal suffrage which would instantly double the electorate. Parliament had shown itself receptive to the gradual addition of new voters; it was alleged that the step by step approach gave each additional group of voters time to understand their new responsibility and become assimilated into the electorate. More important to Parliament was the opportunity to gauge the effect each extension of the franchise made on the political distribution of votes.

On 28 February 1908 a Women's Enfranchisement Bill passed its second reading in the House of Commons. The Liberal Prime Minister, Campbell-Bannerman, was a supporter of woman suffrage and the vote had been overwhelmingly in favour of the Bill, with 273 for and 94 against. Then on 6 April, only two weeks before his death, Campbell-Bannerman resigned and Henry Asquith, then Chancellor of the Exchequer, took over. Asquith was an avowed Anti; his wife had been one of the 104 signatories of the 1889 'Appeal'. The new Prime Minister immediately announced that there was not enough time in the current session of Parliament to discuss the Bill; but the Bill would be discussed at some time during the course of the Parliament's life, i.e. during the next four years, when the Government intended to introduce a Bill to reform the male franchise. There it was — the Antis' old political trick — blocking woman suffrage by linking it with the extension of the male franchise. The female suffragists organized massive processions in protest and the suffragettes began their campaign of ever-increasing violent action. The battle was on.

On 21 July 1908 the Women's National Anti-Suffrage League held its inaugural meeting at the Westminster Palace Hotel in London. An executive committee of eighteen was elected, with the key positions held by Lady Jersey (chairman); Mrs Humphry Ward (chairman of the literature committee) and Gertrude Bell (hon. secretary). At this meeting Mrs Ward declared that in view of 'the spectacle of marchings and counter-marchings, alarums and excursions on behalf of the suffrage cause' the Antis must move into action.

Gertrude's friend from her Oxford days, Janet Courtney, also joined the League and wrote later that Gertrude had supported Mrs Ward on anti-suffrage when 'most of us feared Pankhurst militancy was going to wreck most of what professional women had achieved'.

In December 1908 the Men's Committee for Opposing Female Suffrage was launched. Among its first members were Lord Curzon, Lord Cromer, Sir Alfred Lyall and Gertrude's father, Sir Hugh Bell. The Antis came from both sides of the political divide, but many shared membership of that select and élite 'club' — the University of Oxford. As in the 1889 'Appeal' strong support for anti-suffrage came from the university; in 1908 its clearest exposition was given by the Vinerian Professor of English Law, Albert Venn Dicey.

As a young man Dicey and many of his Oxford contemporaries espoused the political doctrines of Utilitarianism and were influenced by its leading light, J.S. Mill. 'Under his guidance we favoured every attempt to extend not only the liberty but also the political rights of women', wrote Dicey in a 1909 article entitled 'Letters to a friend on votes for women'. These 'Letters' contain a lengthy exposition of the views held by the Antis at that time.

Dicey had no doubts that women should enjoy the fullest civil rights, but as far as political rights were concerned, he stated unequivocably: 'The State has been built up by men; its welfare depends on the encouragement of manly qualities'. He resorted repeatedly to this familiar distinction made by the Antis between 'manly' and 'womanly' qualities. He stated:

Woman . . . compared with a man of equal ability may have a better eye for circumstances around her, but has less foresight. She has assuredly also less of tenacity. . .nor can it be forgotten that women are physically, and probably mentally weaker than men.

These views should not be dismissed as blind bigotry. Serious and scientific debate on the qualities and susceptibilities of the female mind had taken place throughout the nineteenth century whenever there were moves to provide higher education for women. It was maintained that women were unsuited to the stress and content of higher education because of the nature of female biology — women were physically, mentally and emotionally weaker than men. The supporters of the campaign for higher education for women brushed aside these arguments of biological differences between the sexes. And curiously many of the supporters of that campaign, including Dicey, are to be found among the anti-suffragists, adopting the views on biological differences which had previously belonged to their opponents in the debate on women's higher education.

As in the education debate scientists were brought to testify on the nature of women. A book entitled *The Position of Woman: actual and ideal*, published in 1911, contained a collection of seven papers looking at different aspects of its subject. The first, by the professor of Natural History in the University of Aberdeen and his wife, brought forward the latest scientific evidence in considering woman's position biologically. Their conclusion was 'that attempts to lessen the old-fashioned natural differences are to be regarded with extreme suspicion'. The book began and ended with comments from the eminent physicist, Oliver Lodge. He gave the usual reasons for opposing woman suffrage: women were better qualified to exercise civic and not political rights; they already had political influence; and most importantly:

At the present moment the stability of the State is in serious danger. The Party system. . .seems to be on the verge of breaking down. . . . I should be reluctant to add to existing dangers such a leap in the dark as would be involved in the addition to the register of a mass of untried voters.

Dicey also regarded it as 'no slight evil' to introduce large numbers of new electors who had no political training or traditions and did not have 'the independence due to possession of property, or intelligence due to education'. Educated women already enjoyed political influence and civil rights, why risk opening the doors to the uneducated masses?

This was surely the argument against woman suffrage that Gertrude found especially convincing. She held a very low opinion of the majority of women, even when they were her social equals. Her closest friends were men. And later, when she was working in the Middle East, she was conspicuously intolerant of the wives of her colleagues. Although Gertrude thrived among men there was nothing she longed for more than domestic bliss, as wife and mother. Serving alongside Gertrude on the first committee of the Anti-Suffrage League was a prime example of such marital success — Mrs Harrison, mother of five, wife of the philosopher Frederic Harrison.

Frederic Harrison was one of Dicey's Oxford contemporaries who had also fallen under the influence of J.S. Mill but by the turn of the century was prominent among the British philosophers who followed the positivist tradition of Comte. In 1908 Harrison wrote: 'Positivism is intensely conservative as to the distinctive quality with which civilisation has ever invested women, whilst it is ardently progressive in its aim to purify and spiritualise the social functions of women'. Positivism gave the Antis an added intellectual respectability.

Both Dicey and Harrison acknowledged the important part women played in their lives, as did Curzon and Cromer. Cromer told Gertrude in 1914 that 'history shows that all the most distinguished men in the world have been those who have had clever mothers'. But Cromer never denied that the natural differences were immutable. In Cromer's authorized biography his opposition to woman suffrage was explained as 'based on his reverence for women as such. . .he dreaded the consequences of any successful attempt to break down the barrier which Nature herself had imposed between the sexes'.

Gertrude showed no respect for that 'natural barrier', and it is probably easiest to understand her active participation in the anti-suffrage movement when we look at her relationship with those who featured most prominently in it. Cromer and Lyall were much admired by Gertrude — she had dedicated a book to each of them; her own much adored father lent his name to the cause; the Bell family 'intimates' in London society formed the hard core of female supporters; her aunt Maisie became one of the leading London hostesses who helped raise funds for the movement; her closest friend from her Oxford days, Janet Courtney, joined the League; and indeed Gertrude was nurtured in a university that produced the League's leading lights, both male and female. Furthermore, her family was connected with other leading industrialist families who provided prominent members to the anti-suffrage movement: J.A. Pease, the Liberal politician, an active Anti in Parliament and member of the Pease family coal and iron industry (established, like Bell Brothers, in the north-east of England); Violet Markham, a friend of Gertrude and later a distinguished public servant, daughter of that Charles Markham who was managing director of the Stavely Coal and Iron Company.

Gertrude was among friends. There can be no doubt that she shared their social values. Janet Courtney recalled that Gertrude always 'preserved the strictest social etiquette' even when confronted with the vicissitudes of the Middle East. She was able to produce Paris gowns from her baggage when she emerged from the desert. And in the desert she had fine linen for her table, silver cutlery and cut-glass goblets. Gertrude always pined for the comfort of family life and domesticity when far away, and wherever she was Gertrude always deferred to the views of her parents. Of course she was an exceptional woman but she was not a rebel. She shared the conventional attitudes of her upper-class friends and indeed must have sorely felt the stigma of remaining unmarried among a group who regarded a spinster as a 'social failure'. There can be no doubt that the Anti-Suffrage League was Gertrude's natural political home.

From the first, Gertrude threw herself into the organization of the Women's National Anti-Suffrage League. In October 1909 she told her stepmother that she

> went straight to the office and had an interview with a very capable lady who used to be the organising secretary of one of the Suffrage societies and has seen the error of her ways and wants to work for us. I fancy she will make an excellent and very sensible speaker and I intend to follow the matter up.

Gertrude was privy to the political machinations when the Men's Committee and Women's League merged in late 1910. The new National League for Opposing Woman Suffrage came under the chairmanship of Lord Cromer. Gertrude won a great deal of respect during the tense negotiations which preceded the merger. Cromer wrote to Curzon describing Gertrude as 'the cleverest, most sensible and, I may add, the most friendly amongst the women'.

Gertrude seems to have been active in the League over the next two or three years. In February 1912 the League held its most

51

important meeting in the Royal Albert Hall in London. The meeting was addressed by Gertrude's friend Violet Markham, whose speech was hailed a great success. Gertrude had been involved in some of the organization of this meeting. And it had been suggested that her father help Lord Curzon with his contribution to the meeting, but Cromer wrote a very revealing letter to Curzon on the subject:

> I strongly recommend you not to have Sir Hugh Bell. I know him well. He is the great Iron master at Middlesbrough, a strong Free Trader and a very clever man, with a phenomenal power of talking. He is a Liberal, in so far that he votes Liberal, but like a good many other Liberals, all his ideas are strongly Conservative. . . . Moreover, he would be entirely in the pocket of his daughter Miss Gertrude Bell. . . . She is an extremely clever woman, who has travelled a great deal in the East, and written books, one of which she dedicated to me. She has not got much judgment and has a tongue.

The organization of the National League was firmly in Cromer's hands and the one-time autocratic British agent in Egypt was clearly irritated by Gertrude's forceful personality. She seems to have made the north-east her power base and in November 1912 complained to Domnul that 'life was nearly wrecked for a month by arranging an anti-suffragist meeting in Middlesbrough on the largest scale. It was interesting, but it took an appalling amount of time'.

1912 also showed an increase in activity on the part of the suffragettes. Their militancy adversely affected the cause of woman's suffrage and the Antis enjoyed a surge of support in Parliament. As the suffragettes' frustration mounted so did their militant actions. In October 1913 Gertrude recounted to her father details of events at a party at the home of Lady Glenconner, a leading London political hostess and supporter of anti-suffrage:

> Just before I arrived (as usual) 4 suffragettes set on Asquith and seized hold of him, whereupon Alec Laurence in fury seized two of them, twisted their arms until they shrieked. Then one of them bit him in the hand till he bled. And when he told me the tale he was steeped in his own gore.

Within a fortnight of this party Gertrude was heading east — her sights set on the Rashid capital, Ha'il. Her involvement with the anti-suffrage movement was at an end. Soon the outbreak of the First World War would distract the conflicting parties. Many Antis felt forced by the remarkable war effort of women of all classes to reassess their views on woman suffrage. In 1916 Violet Markham announced her intention to join the suffragists. Violet notes in her autobiography, written after Gertrude's death, that this 'recantation, happily for me, made no difference in my ties with Gertrude Bell. . . . She had always taken a rather cynical view of the votes for women campaign'. So it seems that Gertrude's views on the subject did not change, although in Elizabeth Burgoyne's biography of Gertrude she reports being told by Janet Courtney that Gertrude was 'much later on in her life amused by her earlier attitude to anti-suffrage'. But it should be remembered that it was common practice, after woman suffrage had been accepted and had shown itself to have little effect on the body politic, for the Antis to obliterate all memory of their involvement in the anti-suffrage campaign. Their autobiographies often contain no mention of their commitment to the National League. Perhaps Janet Courtney is doing no more than excusing Gertrude from a campaign that in retrospect seemed so absurd. Violet Markham, who saw Gertrude within a year of her death, would surely have told us if Gertrude had ever changed her opinions on anti-suffrage.

Gertrude's active participation in the anti-suffrage movement only lasted a few years. By the end of 1912 it was already of declining interest to her. In the letter she wrote to Domnul describing her involvement in the Middlesbrough anti-suffrage meeting, she continued:

My preoccupation now is Asiatic Turkey. What will happen now that Ottoman prestige has vanished into thin air?. . . I should not be surprised if we were to see, in the course of the next ten years, the break-up of the empire in Asia also the rise. . . of Arab autonomies.

It was a preoccupation that would dominate and devour her life.

6 Love and War

Whatever Gertrude did in her life she did with complete commitment and total conviction. And when her eastern travels brought her into contact with a man she could love then that love grew into an obsession.

They first met in May 1907, when Gertrude was passing through Konia on her way to Maden Sheher where she was going to work with Ramsay. She wrote to Domnul:

> You know there is an English v.consul here now, a charming young soldier with quite a pleasant little wife. He is the more interesting of the two, a good type of Englishman, wide awake and on the spot, keen to see and learn. Will you tell Willie T. I congratulate him on the appointment.

The vice-consul was Charles Hotham Montagu Doughty-Wylie, known as Richard or Dick to his friends. Gertrude stayed a few days in Konia with him and his wife Lillian after completing work with Ramsay. There is little doubt that they maintained friendly contact over the next few years. Although there are no letters extant of this period Gertrude did keep a press cutting of Dick's heroic action in April 1909 at Adana. She always showed a keen interest in Turkish politics and closely followed developments in the region after the success of the Young Turks in 1908. She no doubt followed the career of Doughty-Wylie with equal interest.

By 1909 his consulate in Konia had become responsible for the district known as Cilicia, and this included the town and vilayet of Adana. The district as a whole contained a large number of Armenians — more than 175,000 — and although outnumbered by Muslims by three to one, the Christian Armenians believed that this region should form part of an independent Armenia. The Young Turks' rise to power in 1908 gave the Armenians hope that their national aspirations would be recognized. The Armenians infuriated the local Muslim population with their obvious intentions to gain political dominance in the region and the Muslims reacted with violent attacks on Armenian communities. In Adana a raging mob descended on the Christian quarter. Doughty-Wylie assembled a half-company of Turkish soldiers and led an assault on the mob, though wounded in the arm with a bullet. A massacre was prevented but it was not the end of such ugly incidents. From Adana massacres spread through the vilayet and into northern Syria — more than 20,000 people were killed before the authorities finally brought the mobs under control. For his action Captain Doughty-Wylie was awarded the CMG (Companion of the Order of St Michael and St George) and promoted to the post of consul-general at Addis Ababa.

There remains no evidence of any correspondence between Gertrude and Dick over the next four years. The nature of their relationship does not emerge until 1913 when dramatic events in the Balkans forced changes in Dick's career.

Dick had remained in Ethiopia until the autumn of 1912 when the Balkan War drew him back to Turkey. He became chief director of the Red Cross units on the Turkish side, and his wife worked with him in organizing an emergency hospital in Constantinople. The Turks had only just ended their war with Italy when they now found the province of Macedonia under attack from the recently formed Balkan League. The members of the League — Bulgaria, Serbia, Greece and Montenegro — had formed an alliance to annex Macedonia from Turkish control. Montenegro and Serbia also had designs on Albania, which had only just gained its autonomy by waging war on the Young Turks. Indeed it was probably Albania's military success against the Turks which encouraged the Russian-sponsored Balkan League to launch its own attack on the Turkish provinces of Macedonia and Thrace.

Attempts to end the Balkan War took place in December 1912 in London. The League agreed to allow the Great Powers to decide the frontiers of Albania, but the League members were soon fighting among themselves for the spoils gained from Turkey. And in June 1913 a second Balkan war broke out with the Bulgarians launching an attack on their Serb and Greek allies. In July, as this war was drawing to a close, Doughty-Wylie was recalled to London. It had been decided that he would be sent to Albania as chairman of the committee that was responsible for establishing the Greek–Albanian frontier.

Soon after Dick arrived in England Gertrude invited him to Rounton. His wife was not with him.

After his visit to Rounton, Dick took up residence in his 'old bachelor quarters in Half Moon Street, no. 29'. He wrote to Gertrude:

> I am so glad you took me to Rounton. . . I've always since those Turkey days, wanted to be a friend of yours. Now I feel as if we had come closer, were really intimate friends. I must write something to show, if I can, how very proud I am to be your friend.

Dick's wife Lillian, whom he called Judith, was still away and so he and Gertrude could correspond freely without fear of their intimate letters being read by Judith. It seems that before Dick's visit to Rounton their letters held no secrets but now their relationship was quickly changing. On 22 August Dick wrote:

> Yes for a little time we are alone, but it is only a little time. Judith, knowing you well, and having always before seen your letters, would find it very odd to be suddenly debarred them, and on voyages one lives at close quarters.

The second Balkan War had been brought to an end on 10 August and Dick was now preparing himself for his job in Albania — and separation from Gertrude. On 23 August he wrote:

> And so closes our little time alone. No, it doesn't for we shall still meet in thoughts and fancies; only I shall read no more letters (after perhaps two) from you yourself to me myself no more in the mornings in Half Moon Street. . . . My dear, if I can't write to you, I shall always think of you telling me things in your room at Rounton, showing me something of your mind and something of mine.

At this time Gertrude was still at Rounton and writing daily to Dick. None of her letters survive — Dick burnt them before leaving for Albania: 'Tonight I shall destroy your letters — I hate it — but it is rightful. One might die or something, and they are not for any soul but me.'

Was this to be the sum total of their romance — a few days together at Gertrude's family home and a love affair confined to pen and paper, and now in part reduced to ashes?

As Dick made final preparations to leave for Albania he looked forward eagerly to the challenge of his new job. His romance with Gertrude would soon be behind him:

> And tomorrow we go to the new adventure. To go, to go, I wonder if you or I could not feel a certain pleasure, a certain something now to be satisfied. It is a charming thing, a new adventure.

Gertrude also made plans for a new adventure — but not with excitement and enthusiasm. Her adventure would be an escape from the agony she felt of unfulfilled love. She was forty-five, desperately in love and wretched in her spinsterhood. She set course for Ha'il, the capital of the Rashid family. It was a treacherous journey, made all the more so by the unpredictable, blood-lusting disposition of the Rashids themselves.

She was still in contact with Dick and wrote to him of her plans. He feared she might in her present mood be reckless and in October wrote: 'Please, my dear Gertrude, remember that you said you would run no risks, other than the fair risks which come by the way'.

On 21 November she arrived in Beirut at the very beginning of her expedition and sent Dick a telegram. He immediately wrote to her, recalling again the time they spent together at Rounton and taking up a theme that would constantly recur in their correspondence — whether they should fulfil their sexual desires:

> It's late, and I'm all alone, and thinking of those things, of philosophy and love and life — and an evening at Rounton — and what it all meant . . . . You are in the desert, I am in the mountains, and in these places much could be said under the clouds. Does it mean that the fence was folly, and that we might have been man and woman as God made us and been happy . . . . And I have always maintained that this curious, powerful sex attraction is a thing right and natural and to be gratified, and if it is not gratified what then; are we any worse? I don't know.

Gertrude immersed herself in preparations for her journey into the desert and her letters home to her family were preoccupied with her forthcoming travels:

> The position is this: As far as I can make out. . . there never was a year more favourable for a journey into Arabia than this. The desert is absolutely tranquil and there should be no difficulty whatever in getting to Hayil, that is Ibn al Rashid's capital and even much further . . . . As far as I can make out we shall need 17 camels. . . and they cost an average of £13 a piece including their gear. Bassan says I must reckon to spend £50 on food to take with us, £50 more for presents such as cloaks, keffeyehs for the head. . . I ought to take £80 with me and to give £200 to the Nejd merchant who lives here in return for a letter of credit which will permit me to draw the sum in Hayil. . . a total of £601. . . I am practically using all my next years income for this journey. . . Bassan has all the news of the desert, he knows exactly what I am doing and he is sure to know more or less where I am. But don't go to him with questions unless news of me is greatly overdue.
>
> Dearest beloved father don't think me very mad or very unreasonable and remember always that I love you more than words can say, you and Mother.

It was to her dearest friend Domnul that she wrote revealing her deepest emotions as she set out on the lonely journey to Ha'il:

> I want to cut all links with the world, and that is the best and wisest thing to do. The road and the dawn, the sun, the wind and the rain, the camp fire under the stars, and sleep, and the road again — we'll see what they can do. If they don't cure, then I know of nothing that can. And I have begun to look forward to it — so don't think I'm going off on a wild and desperate adventure in the hope that it may be desperate. It is. quite reasonable for an adventure, and yet exciting enough to divert me. Oh, Domnul if you knew the way I have paced backwards and forwards along the floor of hell for the last few months, you would think me right to try for any way out. I don't know that it is an ultimate way out, but its worth trying. As I have told you before, it is mostly my fault, but that does not prevent it from being an irretrievable misfortune — for both of us. But I am turning away from it now, and time deadens even the keenest things.

Gertrude might have hoped to distance herself from all the torment her love brought her but she certainly did not turn away and end the affair. Even as she prepared her camels for the journey to Ha'il she sent Dick a book filled with her writings of love and devotion. He was now staying at his family home, Theberton Hall in Suffolk. Judith had for some reason fallen out with his family and did not go along to Theberton Hall. Dick in his solitude could freely read of Gertrude's love and write to her:

> Every night I read your book — and love you for it, and want you, but cannot write — not even tonight — no — there is too much to say. I'll read your book and tell your ghost the things which run in my blood — just whisper them, or in some heavenly case, signal them wordless.

, And so he continued to write with ever-increasing passion. Perhaps before Gertrude left for Ha'il she could confess to Domnul that the affair 'was mostly my fault', but now as she enters the desert wastes Dick shows mounting passion and returns again and again to the possibility of a sexual relationship:

> I shall never be your lover, my dear, never. I read that beautiful and passionate book, and know it. Never your lover, that is man to woman . . . . But what we can have, we will keep and cherish. Yes, we will be wise and gentle as you said.

The day after he wrote these words Gertrude went into the desert. But she still did not turn away from the love that tortured her. Throughout her journey to Ha'il Gertrude kept a personal diary for the man she loved. Day by day she spoke to him through the pages of the diary. It began on 16 January 1914:

> Today I returned to the desert. . . crossing the little thread of rail that binds us here to the outer world. . . I have cut the thread. I can hear no more from you or from anyone. . . the only thread which is not cut is that which runs through this little book, which is the diary of my way kept for you.

All the following extracts describing her journey to Ha'il are taken from the diary she kept for Dick. There was another letter diary kept for her family and although it contains more details of events it gives no reflection of her state of mind. Throughout her life the letter diaries and letters that she wrote to her family were in a sense sterile — Gertrude very rarely exposes her inner self in those family letters. And yet, because there are so many of those letters still extant, her life is regarded as well-documented by all who write about her. In a sense this is true — we know a great deal about where she went, what she did. But only in a few personal letters to Domnul and in the diary to Dick do we directly face the emotional character of Gertrude Bell. It was in the diary to Dick that she expressed grave misgivings as to the value of the trip to Ha'il. She complained that the adventure itself gave insufficient intellectual satisfaction, it was the thrill of archaeological discovery that she yearned for. You can sense the excitement when she did actually find a ruined castle, just a few days after setting out into the desert:

> Here stands the last of the castles, Qasr Baîr, very much ruined, and never visited by anyone but Carruthers, who did not even photograph it. It is great fun making the first — and probably the last — record of it.

But while making a plan of the castle she found

> a new grave among the castle walls . . . . The red cotton keffiyyeh and a bit of cotton clothing, thrown down on the stones that covered the grave, were steeped in blood. Occasionally I wonder whether I shall come out of this adventure alive. But the doubt has no shadow of anxiety in it — I am so profoundly indifferent.

Her doubts of 'coming out of this adventure alive' were to be severely tested within the next few weeks. She arrived at Ha'il on 26 February. The Amir was away leading his army against northern tribes and he had left his uncle Ibrahim in charge. Gertrude soon found herself under house arrest and running out of money — Ibrahim had refused to honour the letter of credit for £200 which Gertrude had obtained from the Nejd merchant in Damascus.

There must have been real fear among the Rashid family that Gertrude had come to spy on them. In the Amir's absence there was obviously a lack of authority in Ha'il. Gertrude learnt from the gossip brought to her in her captivity that 'the hand which has pulled the strings in all this business is that of the Amir's grandmother, Fatima, of whom Ibrahim stands in deadly fear. In Ha'il murder is like the spilling of milk'.

After five days captivity Gertrude briefly recorded the experience:

I feel as if I had lived through a chapter of the Arabian Nights during this last week. The Circassian women and the slaves, the doubt and anxiety, Fatima weaving her plots behind the qasr walls, Ibrahim with his smiling lips and restless shifting eyes — and the whole town waiting to hear the fate of the army which has gone up with the Amir against Jof. And to the spiritual sense the place smells of blood. The tales round my camp fire are all of murder. It gets on your nerves when you sit day after day between high mud walls.

And so she sat and waited. Occasionally there were meetings with Ibrahim and also with the chief eunuch Sa'id — 'none more powerful than he'. But Gertrude never boasted much patience and her level of indignation and irritation led her to demand an audience with Sa'id. She spoke to the chief eunuch 'with much vigour, and ended the interview abruptly by rising and leaving him. . .that evening Sa'id arrived with a bag of gold and full permission to go where I liked and when I liked'.

She spent the next day photographing everything at Ha'il and then took her caravan across the desert to Baghdad. But with Ha'il only nine days behind her she was already reflecting on what had passed and was making plans for her next adventure:

Ha'il gave me a sinister impression. I do not like the rule of women and eunuchs. . .I think the Rashids are moving towards their close. Not one grown man of their house remains alive — the Amir only 16 or 17, and all the others are little more than babies, so deadly has been the family strife. I should say the future lies with Ibn Sa'ud. . . I do not know what Ibn Sa'ud is like, but worse he cannot be. So there! My next Arabian journey shall be to him. I have laid out all my plans for it.

But first she had to get to Baghdad. In the desert there was always the constant fear of raids by unfriendly tribes. Travelling with her were rafiqs from different tribes, each providing protection against attack from their own tribe. But it was spring and all the tribes were now in the desert seeking out pasture for their flocks.

Early on the following morning we sighted tents and our rafiqs were reduced to a state of quivering alarm . . . . One of them, however, was induced to ride up to the tents, which he found to be those of an allied tribe. He brought back two new rafiqs for he and his companion flatly refused to go on. So we rode on for 6 hours or so and then again sighted tents. . .the rafiqs even talked of turning back and leaving us. But again we made one of them go up and enquire what Arabs they were and as great good luck would have it they were the Ghazalat who are the only people of any real importance and authority in these parts. We camped with them and took on an excellent rafiq . . . . With him we have felt comparatively safe, but if we had not had him with us we should have been stripped to the skin twice in these last two days.

She reached Baghdad late in March 1914 without further incident and wrote to Dick:

The adventure always leaves one with a feeling of disillusion—don't you know it . . . . Dust and ashes in one's hand, dead bones that look as if they would never rise and dance — it's all nothing, and one turns away from it with a sigh, and tries to fix one's eyes on the new thing before one. This adventure hasn't been successful either, I haven't done what I meant to do. But I have got over that now. It's all one, and I don't care. Already I want the next thing, whatever it may be — I've done with that.

The experience of her travels had affected Gertrude deeply. From Baghdad she wrote to Domnul:

You will find me a savage, for I have seen and heard strange things, and they colour the mind . . . . But whether I can bear with England — come back to the same things and do them all over again — that is what I sometimes wonder . . . . This letter is only for you — don't hand it on to anyone, or tell anyone that the me they knew will not come back in the me that returns. Pehaps they will not find out.

Before returning to England Gertrude went and stayed in Constantinople. She wrote home reassuring letters to her family but as usual they did not reveal her true state, emotional or physical. Her friend Flora Russell, who was in Constantinople at the time, witnessed that Gertrude was completely exhausted and attributed her vivid and cheerful letters home as 'being for the benefit of her family'.

Gertrude returned to England in May and spent much of the summer at Rounton. Dick was still consul-general at Addis Ababa, and was clearly unwilling to leave Judith and set up home with Gertrude. That was not a decision he could take lightly — such action would have brought scandal upon him and ruin his professional career. Furthermore Dick does show a clear religious conviction which might have made him seriously consider his marriage vows to his wife.

Gertrude could scarcely look to the future with much enthusiasm. Perhaps another adventure — a visit to Ibn Sa'ud — perhaps another book to be written. But events in Europe would soon overtake their lives.

There had been an uneasy peace since the end of the Balkan Wars. Serbia and Austria were left the bitterest enemies. It was Austro-Hungarian pressure that succeeded in creating a secure Albania; this prevented land-locked Serbia expanding into Albania and gaining access to the Adriatic Sea.

On the morning of 28 June 1914 an attempt was made to assassinate Archduke Francis Ferdinand, heir to the Hapsburg throne. The conspirators were Bosnian youths dedicated to Serbian nationalism. One of them threw a bomb at the Archduke's car as he drove through the streets of Sarajevo. It missed and exploded under another car. In the afternoon of the same day the Archduke was again driven through the streets of Sarajevo. One of the young Bosnians aimed two shots and mortally wounded Francis Ferdinand and his wife.

Within three weeks Austria had issued an ultimatum to Serbia including a demand that Serbia submit to Austrian supervision.

On 25 July Serbia mobilized its army. On 28 July Austria declared war and bombed Belgrade the next day. The Austro-Serbian war could not be contained.

The Austro-Hungarian–German alliance necessitated German mobilization. The Russians mobilized, regarding Austria's confrontation with Serbia as a direct threat to themselves. The Germans were determined to deal swiftly with France and Belgium before Russia completely mobilized. Germany declared war on France on 3 August and invaded Belgium. Britain had a treaty with Belgium and issued an ultimatum — on 4 August war was declared.

Within just six days the whole of Europe had hurtled headlong into war.

Everyone had expected the war to be concluded within weeks and after two months of continuous conflict all parties looked for new allies. The Germans persuaded the Turks to attack Russia and enter the war in October 1914. Dick with his knowledge of Turkey was recalled to England. It is not known whether he and Gertrude met at this time. But Gertrude soon left England for war-work in France.

In November Gertrude agreed to go to Boulogne to help organize the Red Cross office for tracing the missing and wounded. It was meticulous and demanding work that occupied all her waking hours. This work in Boulogne brought her an immediate awareness of the horrors perpetrated in the war. She visited casualties in the nearby hospital and heard firsthand of life in the trenches. But for all the horror, her work in Boulogne was an escape — an escape from personal torment. Towards the close of 1914 she wrote to Domnul:

> I shall not come to England for the present. At any rate I can work here all day long — it makes a little plank across the gulf of wretchedness over which I have walked this long time. Sometimes even that comes near breaking point . . . . There are days when it is still almost more than I can bear — this is one of them, and I cry out to you, though it is no good.

As long as she could bury herself in her work there was some relief from the misery that her love for Dick brought her. Gertrude did not want to return to England but she did feel that

64

perhaps she had a duty to be at home at this time helping her stepmother cope with the twenty convalescents that were living at Rounton. 'Please telegraph and I'll come at once' was the message she sent home. Two weeks later she wrote:

Do you mind my being here, dearest father. I feel as if I had flown to this work as one might take to drink, for some kind of forgetting that it brings, but, you know it, there's no real forgetting and care rides behind one all the day.

Dick was still in London. He had become involved with the plans for attacking Turkey itself. British forces had already been promptly moved into Shatt al Arab, initially to protect the oilfields on the Persian Gulf, but the campaign soon grew into a massive military expedition.

Gertrude was clearly excited by these developments in the Middle East. She wrote in December to Domnul:

If only I were arriving in Mesopotamia at this moment! I do so long to hear of the occupation of Baghdad. You will see there will be little opposition. I expect Sayid Talib of Basrah knuckled under — I always thought he would; but I pine for details.

She wrote a month later again to Domnul still asking for information on the Mesopotamian expedition. This letter also contained a despairing view of the war — a war that had raged for just four months and would continue for four more years.

The waste, the sorrow of it all . . . . No human skill or valour can break through the defences on either side. Here we sit, and lives run out like water with nothing done. It is unbelievable now at the front — the men knee-deep in water in the trenches, the mud impassable . . . . There is no chance for an officer of the line but that he should be reasonably well wounded and sent home. That is what happens to the lucky ones.

At this time Dick and Gertrude maintained a regular correspondence with each other. In January 1915 a letter to Dick reveals the intensity of Gertrude's feelings:

You fill my cup, this shallow cup that has grown so deep to hold your love and mine. Dearest, when you tell me you love me and want me, my heart sings — and then weeps for longing to be with you. I have filled all the hollow places of the world with my desire for you; it floods out to creep up the high mountains where you live.

Within a month they would be together in London. She had been summoned back to sort out the London Red Cross office for tracing the wounded and missing. Dick had now joined Sir Ian Hamilton's staff and was involved in the preparations for the Gallipoli invasion. Because he knew Turkish Dick specially requested to be among the first to land on the Gallipoli peninsula. He left for Turkey on 23 February. The previous four days had been spent in London — most of the time with Gertrude. She wrote to Dick on 26 February:

I cant sleep — I cant sleep. Its one in the morning of Sunday. I've tried to sleep, every night it becomes less and less possible. You, and you, and you are between me and any rest; but out of your arms there is no rest. Life, you called me, and fire — I flame and am consumed. Dick, its not possible to live like this . . . . Before all the world, claim me and take me and hold me for ever and ever. That's the only way it can be done . . . . Do you think I can hide the blaze of that fire across half the world? or share you with any other?. . . When this thing is over, your work well done, will you risk it all for me? Its that or nothing. I can't live without you . . . . Trust me, believe me. I will delight you. Night and morning and at high noon you shall take me . . . If you love me, take me in this way — if you only desire me for an hour, then have that hour, and I will have it and meet the bill . . . . And if you die, wait for me — I'm not afraid of that other crossing; I will come to you.

It is strange to read Gertrude's reference to the afterlife at the close of her letter. She, a lifelong atheist, now considers committing suicide to join Dick should he be killed. There can be little doubt that Dick believed in an afterlife. Gertrude had often referred to his religious commitment — when she stayed with the Mackinnons in Damascus in 1914 she wrote to Dick: 'So here I am with these kind people — remember them in your prayers'.

And on the same journey, when she came across an unburied body left for the dogs to eat:

> I could not get him from my thoughts, the dead man lying on the great plains . . . . Perhaps now that I have handed him over to you, you will exorcise him.

Dick was horrified at Gertrude's suggestion of taking her own life should he die. His wife Judith had made the same promise to him. He wrote to Gertrude:

> My dear, dont (this is what weighs me down) dont do what you talked of — its horrible to me to think of — that's why I told you about my wife — how much more for you — dont do anything so unworthy of so free and so brave a spirit . . . . Was it perhaps some subtle spirit of foreknowledge, that kept us apart in London? As I go now I am sorry and glad, but on the whole glad — the risk to your body, and to your peace of mind and pride of soul.

This was to be his last letter to Gertrude. Their love would remain forever unconsummated.

On 25 April his ship the *River Clyde* was beached at Gallipoli. Half the troops were landed with terrible loss. Dick took command of the attack on the village of Sedd-el-Bahr. The castle on the way to the village was taken and David Hogarth wrote, in his article on Dick in the *Dictionary of National Biography*, that the 'hand-to-hand fighting went on till noon, Doughty-Wylie, armed only with a cane, leading the rushes'. Victory was almost at hand. Dick led his men in a rush on to the summit of their final objective — Hill 141. The Turks fell back. The hill and the whole beach had been won when a bullet hit Dick in the head. He was buried where he fell. For his action at Gallipoli he was posthumously awarded the Victoria Cross.

The whole Gallipoli campaign was a disaster for the British — thousands of men were killed. Gertrude mourned for one man.

For months Gertrude suffered dark despondency. In August she wrote to her stepmother:

It's very dear of you to suggest coming up, but you mustn't do it. Nobody does any good really; it sounds ungrateful but it is so. Nothing does any good.

Three years later she recalled her last meeting with Dick on 22 February 1915:

Oh Father, dearest, do you know that tonight is just 3 years since D and I parted. I can't think why the recurring date should bring back old memories so strongly, but it is so, and I've lived again through the four days three years ago almost minute by minute. . .this sorrow at the back of everything deadens me in a way to all else.

Gertrude continued through 1914 to work in the Red Cross office in London. In October that year she received a letter from David Hogarth. He was based in Cairo organizing a branch of the Admiralty intelligence service dealing with the Arabs. He wanted Gertrude to join him and help prepare detailed information on the location, numbers and lineage of the Arab tribes of northern Arabia. She resolutely declined to go. But a few weeks later she told her friend Janet Courtney, Hogarth's sister: 'I've heard from David; he says anyone can trace the missing but only I can map Northern Arabia. I'm going next week'.

On 30 November 1915 Gertrude arrived in Cairo.

7 Tangled Web

In November 1915 Gertrude began her career with British military intelligence. She had, over the previous ten years, collected a mass of information on the Arabs that was of considerable value to the intelligence service. The question that must be asked is whether she participated in intelligence operations prior to being officially co-opted into the service in November 1915. Had she just been an adventurer and archaeologist or was she also, as the Turks suspected, a British spy? Were any of her journeys really intelligence missions under the cover of adventure and archaeological prospecting?

There is certainly little documented evidence available which reveals any direct relationship with military intelligence in the years prior to 1915. But there is a great deal of circumstantial evidence which suggests that there existed an informal exchange of information — if only at the level of conversation between friends. And it is Gertrude's friends which provide her first link with the intelligence network operating in the Middle East. These friends included:

Aubrey Herbert, a close friend, to be found visiting Gertrude at Rounton in the summer of 1906. He was a member of military intelligence and in 1906 was in the process of preparing a secret guide called a *Military Report on Syria*. Gertrude had returned from Syria just a year earlier.

George Lloyd, a friend and visitor to Rounton. He was a member of military intelligence and, with Herbert, was working on the *Military Report on Syria*.

Denison Ross, a family friend, head of the London School of Oriental Studies and an adviser to military intelligence. He first met Gertrude in September 1898, when he began to teach her Persian and Arabic.

David Hogarth, brother of Gertrude's close friend from Lady Margaret Hall, Janet. An archaeologist, he was the corner-stone of British intelligence operations in the Middle East—liaising between the intelligence service and the archaeologists working for it.

Valentine Chirol, Gertrude's 'dearest Domnul'. A director of the foreign department of *The Times*, he had many highly placed friends in foreign governments. Chirol wielded influence and information.

As early as 1909 she was obviously involved in discussions on eastern politics at a high level. A few months after returning from travels in the Middle East she wrote to her stepmother with reference to the troubles in Turkey:

> When I came in I found a telegram from George Lloyd asking me to lunch today so I rang him up and asked him to dine with me. He came back yesterday. . . Willie T [Tyrell]. . . is coming after dinner. So I shall have a good all round view of the crisis. It is very serious. I should think anything might happen.

Gertrude's desert travels of course brought her into direct contact with many involved in middle-eastern politics. During her travels of 1909 she stayed, in March, with Lorimer, the British resident in Baghdad. She wrote home revealingly:

> (This for the private ear of my family). Mr. Lorimer says that he has never met anyone who is in the confidence of the natives in the way I am, and Mr Lorimer, I should wish you to understand, is an exceptionally able man.

Lorimer took Gertrude up river in a launch to visit Sir William Willcocks — described as 'one of Britain's keenest intelligence brains in the East' in Victor Winstone's book *The Illicit Adventure*.

During these same travels in 1911 she planned to make contact with David Hogarth:

> Tomorrow I go to Carchemish in the hope of finding Mr. Hogarth there. . . .
> Just after I had written to you the kaimmakam came over to call on me and told me that Mr. Hogarth had left but that Mr. Thompson was still at Carchemish. Accordingly I went there — it was only 5 hours' ride — and found Mr. Thompson and a young man called Lawrence (he is going to make a traveller).

Gertrude Bell and T. E. Lawrence.

It was her first meeting with T.E. Lawrence. Although she did not see Hogarth on this occasion there is evidence that her travels brought her into contact with him and also her friend George Lloyd, a British intelligence officer in Constantinople at this time. The evidence of these encounters comes in 1917 when she writes to her father from Mesopotamia. Gertrude is concerned with the well-being of Fattuh, her trusty Armenian servant who accompanied her on her pre-war desert treks:

> Heaven knows if he is still living. Aleppo has suffered and is suffering most horribly from Turkish persecution and I fear his well-known association with George [Lloyd] and Mr. Hogarth and me will put him at a grave disadvantage.

Gertrude's 1911 visit to Carchemish brought her into contact with a whole group of archaeologists who also worked for intelligence. Carchemish itself was not only an archaeological excavation site but also a base for intelligence operations in the area. The men working there — T.E. Lawrence, Campbell Thompson and Leonard Woolley — were all involved in local intelligence and had long been friends. T.E. Lawrence was very much Woolley's protégé; they had first met in Oxford in 1905, when Woolley was assistant keeper of the Ashmolean Museum; David Hogarth was soon to become the Museum's keeper. The Oxford fraternity was at work. And of course even today Oxford and Cambridge are prime hunting-grounds for new recruits to military intelligence.

Gertrude records that the Carchemish archaeologists 'showed me their diggings and their finds and I spent a pleasant day with them'. Did they really talk of nothing else? Gertrude's fascination with eastern politics would have inevitably made it a subject for conversation and exchange of information. A few weeks later she wrote to her stepmother:

> I shall write a long article for some leading journal when I get home, and call it "The Pacification of the Desert", for it should be known how well and wisely the Turks are handling matters here.

On this journey Gertrude had also visited Dr Andrae's German archaeological expedition in Mesopotamia. She spent three days with them in April profiting from 'endless talks with Dr Andrae' and discussions with 'Herr Preusser'. Conrad Preusser was Germany's chief agent on the Euphrates during the First World War. Even the head of the Kaiser's intelligence service, Baron Max von Oppenheim, was an archaeologist.

It was perhaps Gertrude's 1913 expedition to Ha'il that most obviously could have provided valuable intelligence information. She would not have been the first with intelligence interests to visit the Rashids — twenty years earlier the traveller Baron von Nolde, who was known to work for the Tsar's secret service, travelled to Ha'il.

David Hogarth, President of the Royal Geographic Society, gave the Society an account in 1927 of Gertrude's expedition to Ha'il and indicates its value to military intelligence:

> Her journey was a pioneer venture which not only put on the map a line of wells, before unplaced or unknown but also cast much new light on the history of the Syrian desert frontiers. . . . But perhaps the most valuable result consists in the mass of information that she accumulated about the tribal elements ranging between the Hejaz railway on the one flank and the Sirhan and Nefûd on the other, particularly about the Howaitât group, of which Lawrence, relying on her reports, made signal use in the Arab campaigns of 1917 and 1918.
>
> Her stay in Hayil was fruitful of political information especially concerning both the recent history and the actual state of the Rashid house, and also its actual and probable relations with the rival power of the Ibn Sauds. Her information proved of great value during the war.

One of the few documented examples of her pre-1915 intelligence involvement was written only a few weeks after Britain had declared war on Germany. Gertrude sent a letter full of middle-east intelligence to Wyndham Deedes of the Military Operations Directorate; part of this letter was sent to the Under-Secretary of Foreign Affairs, Sir Edward Grey:

> Syria, especially Southern Syria, where Egyptian prosperity is better known, is exceedingly pro-English. . . . On the whole I should say that Iraq would not willingly see Turkey at war with us and would take no active part in it. But out there, the

Turks would probably turn their attention to Arab chiefs who have received our protection. Such action would be extremely unpopular with Arab Unionists who look on Sayid Talib of Basrah, Kuwait, and Ibn Sa'ud, as powerful protagonists. . . . Ibn Sa'ud is most anxious to get some definite recognition from us and would be easy to secure as an ally. I think we could make it pretty hot for the Turks in the Gulf. It is perhaps worth knowing that Lynch's agent in Baghdad, Mr Arthur Tod (an able man) is on the closest terms of intimacy with the leading Arabs of Baghdad. . . . If Turkey went to war it is possible that the Arab Unionists might take that opportunity to throw off the yoke — perhaps they would not take the initiative, but they would not be difficult to direct on those lines. The complication in Syria is that the French have earmarked it and the people want us, not France.

Within a month Turkey had entered the war, and Britain was launching its Mesopotamian expedition. It was more than a year later that Gertrude was officially working for military intelligence but already she was clearly well acquainted with agents like Arthur Tod, and others who kept her informed on Ibn Sa'ud.

When she did finally join the ranks of political officers in the Middle East she was instantly among friends. Upon arrival in Cairo in December 1915 she was met by David Hogarth and T.E. Lawrence. She met regularly with Lawrence and was joined within a few weeks by George Lloyd. Her main work at this time consisted of completing the intelligence files on the tribes of Arabia, with special attention to their numbers and political grouping. But soon she would be involved in formulating policy — Gertrude could not be contained to performing the relatively tame task of filling in intelligence files. In the new year she was off to India to try and encourage cooperation between intelligence departments in India and Egypt. Gertrude also wanted the Viceroy, Hardinge, to sanction the establishment of a permanent intelligence bureau for the Near East. The visit was semi-official and perhaps partly set up by Sir Valentine Chirol, who was working in Delhi for *The Times*. Gertrude knew that her department might refuse to pay her expenses but she was prepared to finance this journey herself.

Gertrude best liked to operate independently, gaining access to the people at the top through her influential friends, thereby

eliminating the formalities of edging gently along 'official chan-
nels'. Hers was a direct and forceful approach which enabled her
to achieve immediate success — as part of a team it would lead her
into all sorts of difficulties with her superiors. Subordination did
not come easily to Gertrude. She had always had direct access to
those in authority and had surely from the time of her first desert
travels, given them the benefit of her knowledge and opinions on
the Arab peoples.

Gertrude's appointment in Cairo in November 1915 was an
extension of a commitment and involvement in middle-eastern
affairs which she had shown for a decade.

8 The Rise of GLB, 1915–1918

Gertrude's arrival in Cairo in November 1915 coincided with major political and military manoeuvrings in the Middle East.

Lord Kitchener, Secretary of State for War, had just arrived in Egypt and was considering the fate of the wretched Dardanelles campaign. Within a few weeks he authorized the withdrawal of British forces. Gertrude wrote home:

> Yes, the retreat from Gallipoli was wonderful. It doesn't bear thinking about. But it was no good staying. Lots of Mediterranean Forces are here now. The tales they tell make one's heart ache — the folly and muddle of it all, and the vain courage.

Kitchener was already eagerly supporting a new military initiative which could improve Britain's flagging position in the Middle East. But despite his enthusiastic support for an attack on Alexandretta, too many obstacles prevented its wide acceptance.

The British were determined to be in a position of ascendanc~ when the Ottoman empire disintegrated, so that they might take control of large areas of the Middle East. But the French also had imperial designs in the region.

Gertrude spent much of her first week in Cairo with Mark Sykes who would shortly leave for England and commence negotiations with the French. Mark Sykes was visiting Cairo to liaise with al-Faruqi, whom the British regarded as the representative of the Sharif of Mecca and of those Arabs who worked through secret societies for an autonomous Arab nation in the Middle East.

Mark Sykes returned to London in December to meet the French delegate Picot. The two men spent the next four months delineating the areas which their respective countries laid claim to. Known as the Sykes–Picot agreement, it attempted to make a tidy arrangement between the British and the French, with some accommodation for Arab aspirations. Within two years the intentions and interpretations of this agreement were in dispute, and the Sharif of Mecca even refused to admit any foreknowledge of the agreement via his representative al-Faruqi. But then, the Sharif had secured himself a very good deal with the British high commissioner to Egypt, Sir Henry McMahon.

During Gertrude's six weeks in Cairo she became a regular visitor at the home of the McMahons. Sir Henry was already involved in negotiations to secure the allegiance of Husain, the Sharif of Mecca. The British were anxious to hasten the collapse of the Ottoman Empire and approached the Sharif to enlist his support in an Arab revolt against the Ottomans. It was the Sharif who could initiate a *jehad*, or holy war, against non-Muslims like the British. It was essential he remain an ally. The Sharif was willing to co-operate with the British but at a price. The lengthy correspondence between McMahon and Husain, from July, 1915 to March, 1916, resulted in guarantees of territory being made to the Sharif. He would take control of the Holy Places of Islam, all of Arabia and some other areas. The McMahon-Husain correspondence would in time, like the Sykes–Picot agreement, was prey to conflicting interpretations.

Gertrude's regular companions in those early weeks in Cairo included old friends like Captain Woolley of Carchemish, T. E. Lawrence and of course David Hogarth. Lawrence was very much under Hogarth's influence and it was Hogarth's opinions that Lawrence adopted and moulded into his own ideas. Gertrude too looked to Hogarth for wisdom on the Middle East and at this time shared his misgivings on the advisability of native Arab government.

Gertrude did not yet hold an official position in Cairo so she could still directly inform highly-placed friends of her own personal assessment of political and military strategy without, as happened in later years, bringing down the wrath of her superiors. A few weeks after arriving in Cairo she wrote to her friend Lord Robert Cecil. He had been responsible for organizing the Red Cross department for wounded and missing, where Gertrude herself had worked immediately prior to leaving for Cairo. Recently he had been appointed as Parliamentary-Under-Secretary for Foreign Affairs. Gertrude wrote him a long letter on the state of middle-eastern affairs:

We are marking time, not very successfully, I fear, in Mesopotamia, and waiting for the Turkish attack on the Canal . . . . It looks as if they were going to tackle the Mesopotamian expedition before they come here, and as far as Egypt is concerned that is most fortunate, for until the last three weeks no preparations had been made to meet them, and the troops in this country were mostly details or raw and quite incoherent masses of Australians . . . . The negotiations with the Sharif have, however, been very skilfully conducted, and as long as we can keep him in play there is no fear of a big religious movement . . . . Meantime we are hampered both by the French and by India, as you know . . . . We could probably come to terms, but never on the basis of relinquishing the whole of Syria — and the demands put forward recently by Picot extended French Syria from the Mediterranean to the Tigris . . . . A serious Arab movement, if it were once to be set on foot, would turn them out of N Africa just as easily as it would turn us out of Egypt . . . . I think they [the French] will have to be content with the Alexandretta corner and Cilicia (good country and a good port) and of course the Lebanon which they will not forego — I think Beyrout also.

The weakness of the argument is that the Arabs can't govern themselves — no one is more convinced of that than I — and when they come to us for help and counsel (as they will) the French will not regard it favourably . . . .

As for the Indian difficulty, the retreat in Mesopotamia may help bring the Indian Government into line. Mesopotamia is far less complicated a question than Syria; it is decades behind Syria in culture, and the Arab unionist movement has scarcely begun there. We shall not be able to annex either of the two provinces, Bastar or Iraq, but no one will object to our administration there if it is not graduated through an Indian bureaucracy — colonisation would have to be very delicately handled!

Gertrude's arrival in Cairo had also coincided with a major British defeat in Mesopotamia, and the Indian government was held responsible for the mismanagement of the campaign, especially in providing insufficient troops and poorly organized supply lines. The Mesopotamian expedition had begun as a small campaign to secure the British presence at Shatt al 'Arab on the Persian Gulf, protecting oil supplies for the navy, but by November, 1915 their sights were set on the capture of Baghdad. Moving up the Euphrates the British army attempted to capture the

Turkish stronghold at Ctesiphon, but were, after three days' confrontation with the Turks, forced to retreat. So, for the moment, the Baghdad adventure ended — but worse was to follow. The retreating army established itself at Kut and was soon surrounded by the Turks. Attempts to relieve Kut would continue over the next few months. The Indian government was blamed for these campaign failures, for it was the Indian Civil Service that was directly in control of all affairs in the Middle East. And those working in Cairo felt it particularly absurd that affairs concerning Arabia fell under Indian and not Egyptian administration.

The conflict between Cairo and India was at its height when on 1 January 1916 Gertrude received two letters from India — one from Domnul, who was working in Delhi for *The Times*, and the other, an invitation from the viceroy, Lord Hardinge. Surely it was Domnul, who had the ear of the viceroy, who had engineered this meeting. Within six weeks Gertrude was in Delhi discussing middle-eastern affairs with Lord Hardinge. He recommended that she went to work at the newly-formed Arab Bureau in Basra helping to liaise with the Indian administration. She wrote home from Delhi on February 18:

> I think I have pulled things straight a little as between Delhi and Cairo. But nothing will ever keep them straight except constant personal intercourse — it ought not be difficult to manage and I am convinced that it is essential.

Lord Hardinge felt he could trust Gertrude to help manage the Arab Bureau in Basra. He had been very reluctant to lose any control over Mesopotamian affairs because he feared that some of the British in the region showed particular sympathy with the Shi'a Muslims. The Shi'a were the majority in Mesopotamia but in India all the Muslims belonged to the other Islamic schism, Sunni. The Sunnis looked to the Sultan as the Caliph of Islam, so they were unwilling to fight the Ottomans, and could easily have been encouraged to revolt in India if the administration was seen to show preferential treatment to Mesopotamian Shi'as.

Gertrude arrived in Basra in early March and stayed with Sir Percy and Lady Cox. He was the chief political officer in the Gulf and much admired by Gertrude. While in India Gertrude had been appointed an editor of the *Gazetteer of Arabia* which was being compiled at Simla in northern India. She continued to work on collecting detailed information on the Arab tribes. Her letters home complained of 'monotonous days'. Everyone yearned for military successes and a march on Baghdad, but Kut was still under siege. An attempt by General Aylmer to relieve Kut a few days after Gertrude's arrival in Basra had failed dismally — Gertrude wrote home: 'The hasty recall of General Aylmer is sufficient comment on recent events'.

She was of course also deeply interested in events on the Western front: 'I wonder what's at the back of Verdun — is it a last great effort or no? Or is it going to succeed still? It drags on so long — a month's battle and no end to it'. At least she could be 'thankful to think that M [Maurice] won't be back in France at any rate till the end of April. The relief it is to know that he is not fighting'. But not all the members of the Bell family shared Gertrude's views on the best place for Maurice during the war: three months later when Maurice had still not left for the war zone Gertrude wrote of her father's 'attempts to get him out to the front, which I devoutly hope will prove fruitless'.

In early May the Mesopotamian expedition suffered a severe setback when the 9,000 British and Indian troops under siege at Kut were forced to surrender. More than 24,000 lives had been lost in the attempts to relieve Kut. Spirits were low in Basra. In the East and in England blame for the campaign failures was apportioned. Gertrude wrote to her father:

I don't hold a brief for the Govt of India, but it is only fair to remember that K [Kitchener] drained India white of troops and of all military requirements, including hospitals and doctors, at the beginning of the war, that the campaign was forced on them *from England*, and that when it developed into a very serious matter — far too big a matter for India to handle if she had had command of her resources — neither troops, nor artillery, nor hospital units, nor flying corps, nor anything were sent back in time to be of use. And what was perhaps still more serious was that all their best Generals had gone to France or Gallipoli, many of them never to return.

Politically, too, we rushed into the business with our usual disregard for a comprehensive political scheme. We treated Mesop as if it were an isolated unit, instead of which it is part of Arabia, its politics indissolubly connected with the great and far reaching Arab question. . . . The co-ordinating of Arabian politics and the creation of an Arabian policy should have been done at home — it could only have been done successfully at home. There was no one to do it, no one who had ever thought of it, and it was left to our people in Egypt to thrash out, in the face of strenuous opposition from India and London, some sort of wide scheme. . . . Well, that is enough of politics. But when people talk of our muddling through it throws me into a passion. Muddle through! why yes so we do — wading through blood and tears that need never have been shed.

Gertrude had become well established in Basra and was responsible for writing a large number of intelligence publications, always signed with the now famous initials GLB. She had also initiated communication with Ibn Rashid 'whom it is rather important to preserve as a neutral if we can do no more'. Taking direct initiative in political events was 'exciting' for Gertrude and much preferred by her to writing reports. She explained to her mother later the same year just how frustrating she found it to be confined to report writing:

I've been busy with a long memorandum about the whole of our central Arabian relations, which I've just finished. It will now go to all the High and Mighty in every part. One can't do much more than sit and record if one is of my sex, devil take it; one can get things recorded in the right way and that means, I hope, that unconsciously people will judge events as you think they ought to be judged. But it's small change for doing things, very small change I feel at times.

Gertrude yearned for power. She must also have envied her friend T.E. Lawrence's involvement in Arab affairs. He had shortly left with Sir Ronald Storrs on a visit to Jidda to negotiate with the Sharif of Mecca. The Sharif had just boldly proclaimed himself King of the Arab countries. The negotiations with him culminated in an Arab revolt which Lawrence supplied directly with bags of gold and ammunition. This was no doubt a role Gertrude yearned for especially as her own dealings with Ibn Rashid had collapsed:

We didn't succeed in roping in Ibn Rashid. Everything that could be done was done; he was forgiven seventy times seven, but he wouldn't listen to our piping.

By May 1916 it became clear that Gertrude would be appointed official correspondent to Cairo. She told her father:

I shall have to come more strictly under official control and I should not be able to leave this country without very good cause shown, like any other person with a job here.

In June the official order came through making her

part of I.E.F. 'D', the Indian Expeditionary Force 'D', and I believe I am to have pay, but fortunately I need not wear uniform! I ought to have white tabs, for I am under the Political Department. It's rather comic isn't it. It has its disadvantages, but I think it is the right thing to do.

The disadvantage of being subject to official control was not one ever to bother Gertrude — as an army political officer she saw herself in a key position for influencing developments in the area. When in August 1916 she was asked by a superior what part she intended to play in the future administration of Iraq she commented that 'I shall have to keep an eye on it . . . I suppose I shall be able to keep an eye on all developments in the Near East through the Arab Bureau.' She was already writing important policy reports which were sent on to Whitehall by Sir Percy Cox.

She worked at a furious pace, even through the blistering heat of the summer. But she did suffer repeated bouts of fever and occasional jaundice, and in the spring of 1917 her hair began to fall out leaving her with not enough 'left to pin a hat to'. In the summer her hair went white. But Gertrude always maintained an amazing preoccupation with her dress throughout the war. She gave a constant stream of detailed orders to her family for hats and gowns to be sent to her. And when the gown she had requested did not arrive, probably because it was stolen at Bombay, she wrote home declaring 'isn't it a tragedy about my black satin gown. Of course it's the very gown I most wanted'. And a month later she was still bemoaning the great loss!

By the summer of 1917 Gertrude was installed in her own house in Baghdad — she described

> a rose garden with three summer houses in it. . . but a kitchen had to be built and a bath room, and sunblinds to put up — a thousand things.

It was Gertrude's first home of her own and she would live in it for the rest of her life.

Her arrival in Baghdad in mid-April had followed soon after the British defeat of the city. The new thrust through Mesopotamia had begun in late 1916 under the command of General Maude. He was given full support by the War Office in London, which had by now taken over charge of the campaign from the Indian authorities. Maude's army was well equipped and had established efficient supply lines. In February 1917 Gertrude was able to report to her family:

> Today we have had the news of the crossing of the Tigris above Kut, which means, I hope, the fall of Kut before long and then probably interesting developments among the tribes who are still hostile. If only all this had happened a year ago! But one realises how impossible it was a year ago, before we had proper transport or equipment.

Indeed within a few days Kut was totally abandoned by the Turks. The military situation in Mesopotamia had been overturned and the Turks were fleeing before the Anglo-Indian army. On March 11 the City of the Caliphs — Baghdad — was in British hands. Two days earlier Gertrude wrote to her father:

> That's the end of the German dream of domination in the Near East — Berlin — Baghdad and all the rest. Their place is not going to be in the sun; it would have been if they had left well alone and not tried to force the pace by war. We had, in my opinion, for all practical purposes resigned this country to them, and they knew it well enough. . . . We shall, I trust, make it a centre of Arab civilisation and prosperity.

In April Gertrude left Basra to journey up river. Nine days later she reached Baghdad. She really rejoiced at arriving there; it was a city she had always loved — full of old friends. And now

she was in at the beginning of the new British administration —
she was immensely excited by this new adventure:

> All my acquaintances and friends have flocked in to see me.
> I've visited the Naqib, the head religious man and ally of many
> years standing, and have been received with open arms. And it
> is all immensely interesting — War Office telegraphing for
> signed articles from me etc etc I'm going to have an exciting
> summer. Sir P [Percy Cox] gives me lots of thrilling things to
> do and is the kindest of chiefs.
> Baghdad is a mass of roses and congratulations.

She took on a massive workload. Her daily routine consisted of
a horse ride from 6 to 7.30 a.m., followed by a bath and breakfast
and then straight to the office where she stayed until seven or
eight in the evening. She spent much of her time interviewing
tribal sheikhs and messengers from the desert, always gathering
and sorting information on the Arab tribes. By the beginning of
July 1917 all the tribes to the north and north-east of Baghdad
were 'alphabetically tabled and beautifully typed in many copies', and then began the work on the tribes of the Euphrates. But
alongside the cataloguing were the political dealings with local
sheikhs. A particular success for Gertrude at this time was a
treaty settled with her 'friend' Fahad Beg of the Anaizah:

> And as soon as he has possessed himself with a set of false teeth
> he sets out to guard the whole western desert for us. It's a great
> haul, one of the most important things we've done, and the
> Turks and Germans are gnashing their teeth. While Fahad had
> been here waiting for his treaty to be completed they have sent
> down two parties of Turkish and German officers, to our
> certain knowledge, with bags of gold to buy his tribesmen in his
> absence. We've beaten them, Fahad stopped a Syrian caravan
> last week by writing to his son in the desert — at my special
> request. And now we ought to hold the frontier.

One can not help but wonder how many bags of gold the
British had to offer Fahad to outbid the Turks and Germans!
Enlisting the support of tribal sheikhs was essential to the
maintenance of law and order in Mesopotamia. The Turkish
control over the region had been very strong and as soon as the

Turks withdrew the whole administration collapsed. The occupying British forces had to set up some sort of administration as quickly as possible. Political officers, like Gertrude, followed in the wake of the conquering army and began dealing with local sheikhs — making them responsible for law and order in their own tribal areas. It was work Gertrude was especially well suited for as she had got to know many of the sheikhs personally on her earlier desert travels.

This system of devolving authority on the sheikhs had the serious disadvantage of placing wealth and power in the hands of a group whose loyalty to the British administration was unreliable. The British were certainly able to gain some degree of loyalty from the Shi'as who had been suppressed under the Turks and subjected to Sunni law. The British swiftly gave authority to Shi'a religious institutions. Gertrude wrote to Domnul of the Shi'a support for the British:

> It is the Shiahs of the Saiyid class who know that they would have least to gain by the return of the Turks — the alienation of the Shi'ahs has been a great asset to us and has meant, for instance, that we never had any religious feeling to contend with in Naj'f and Karbala.

The Turks had not given up hope of reconquering Mesopotamia and intended to build up supplies and men along the Syrian frontier but there were other areas in the Middle East demanding troop reinforcements — most notably, Gaza. Gaza was strategically very important; whoever held Gaza would have access to southern Palestine. The Turks feared that British success in Gaza would enable the British army to capture all of Palestine and then march on Syria. Troops were massed on both sides in Gaza. On 31 October 1917 the British opened fire on the Turkish lines. Within a few days General Allenby broke through the enemy lines and began to march through southern Palestine towards Jerusalem.

With the advance into Palestine came the British government's recognition of Zionist claims — on 2 November the Foreign Secretary, A.J. Balfour, issued the Balfour Declaration, stating that the British Government viewed with favour the establishment in Palestine of a National Home for the Jewish People, and will use their best endeavours to facilitate the achievement of this object.

On 9 December Jerusalem was captured. It took a further nine months before the Turks were finally expelled from the whole of Palestine. During that time the Balfour Declaration was endorsed by all the Allied Powers. But it was not a development in middle-eastern politics that found favour with Gertrude. She wrote home a few weeks after the capture of Jerusalem when it had become clear that Palestine (a district of Ottoman Syria) would eventually fall to the British:

By the way, I hate Mr Balfour's Zionist pronouncement with regard to Syria. It's my belief that it can't be carried out, the country is wholly unsuited to the ends the Jews have in view; it is a poor land, incapable of great development and with a solid two-thirds of its population Mohammedan Arabs who look on Jews with contempt. To my mind it's a wholly artificial scheme divorced from all relation to facts and I wish it the ill-success it deserves — and will get I fancy.

Gertrude had long objected to Zionist claims to Palestine and was much irritated by those in government, like Herbert Samuel, who were attempting to establish a pro-Zionist policy during the first years of the Great War, when dissolution of the Ottoman empire looked feasible. She wrote to Domnul in January 1915:

I had a long and characteristic letter from Lord Cromer. Incidentally he concurred to my view that the Jewish "Kingdom" of Palestine was all moonshine. So Herbert Samuel needn't begin to stitch at his robes yet, nor rub up his Hebrew.

In 1917 Herbert Samuel, former Home Secretary in Asquith's Government, did exercise a direct influence on the government's decision to issue the Balfour Declaration.

Although Gertrude strongly objected to the Zionist principle, she did seem to expect Jews to gain power in Mesopotamia. At this time the religious groupings in Mesopotamia's total population of three million were: 1.5 million Shi'a; 1.1 million Sunni; 87,000 Jews and 79,000 Christians. Most of the Jews, more than

50,000, lived in Baghdad, where there were 50,000 Shi'as and over 100,000 Sunnis. She wrote to her father in November, 1917, soon after the Balfour Declaration:

> I'm going to cultivate the Jewish community and find out more about them. So far I've only met bigwigs, such as the chief Rabbi. There's no doubt they'll be a great power here some day.

In the closing months of 1917 Gertrude was weakened by a succession of fevers and every few weeks she returned to the convalescent hospital for several days' care. She had worked at a phenomenal rate, forever taking on new projects. In mid-November 1917, when she had only just regained some energy from the latest bout of illness, she took over the editorship of the vernacular newspaper *Al Arab*. It was a project she had initiated in June, and her fellow political officer Philby had been appointed official editor, with her Arab friends in Baghdad being given positions on the staff. Gertrude notes that the newspaper was given the name *Al Arab* (The Arab) because it was 'the first paper published under the new order of Arab liberty'.

When Gertrude took over the editorship of *Al Arab* she planned major changes in the newspaper; she was

> full of schemes for making it more alive by getting provincial correspondents and a local news-writer. . . . My public will take more interest in hearing that Ibn so and so was fined for being without a lantern after dark than in the news that an obscure village in Flanders has been bombed.

And so Gertrude devoured another project — as well as all the reports she was writing for Sir Percy and for London. She was burying herself in work; using it as a means of protecting her from time to dwell on the tragedies of the past, the loneliness of the present and the emptiness of the future. She wrote to her father that

> The days melt like snow in the sun. But it's just as well for I've been realising this evening that if I weren't so busy I should be very lonely.

And in another letter home she refers to Baghdad as 'more than a second home now — it's a new life, a new possibility of carrying on existence'. But memories of the past could not be forever suppressed and when she received a letter from an old friend, Beatrice Brownrigg, she was very disturbed by it and unable to reply. She explained to her stepmother:

> I can't answer it. . . . I can't pick up the thread where I dropped it two and a half years ago. And it becomes more, not less, difficult. I'm more and more conscious of being cut off by a wall of agonising experience from what lay before. Even memory scarcely ever goes back or behind it, or only to sicken wearily at the thought of what it's passing over.

Her life now belonged to Mesopotamia and she was, in her own words, 'getting to be rather a dab at Arab politics'. Gertrude was determined to be directly involved in the important political decisions and told her father:

> I want to watch it all very carefully almost from day to day, so as to be able to take what I hope may be something like a decisive hand in final disposition. I shall be able to do that, I shall indeed, with the knowledge I'm gaining.

But the pressure of work and repeated illness took its toll and at the close of 1917 she complained to her father of a

> temporary (let's hope) anaemia of the brain which makes me work so slowly that I never get through my job and bring work home every night to finish after dinner.

Sir Percy saw the strain and Gertrude was sent off on holiday for the first two weeks of 1918. She spent her time motoring along the Euphrates; visiting Babylon on the way back to Baghdad. It was a journey full of memories for her, especially at Babylon. She was reminded there of the warm welcome she had received in 1911 from the German archaeologist Koldewey:

> It's no good trying to think of him as an alien enemy and my heart ached when I stood in the empty, dusty little room where Fattuh used to put up my camp furniture and the Germans and

I held eager conversation over plans of Babylon or Ukhaidir. What a dreadful world of broken friendships we have created between us.

Soon after returning to Baghdad she began plans for a three months holiday in the summer. It was a plan that her doctor, Colonel Wilcox, approved, for Gertrude was clearly still very weak. She hoped to travel to the Persian mountains ending up in Tehran and returning via Isfahan, but these plans were temporarily shelved because she received in February 'terrible accounts of the destitution of the country'. Russian troops, who had been driving the Turks out of Persia, had become totally demoralized during the winter of 1917/18 and by February 1918 were making their way home plundering villages for food and pulling down houses to use the timber as fuel. There was famine throughout north and north-west Persia and Gertrude could not contemplate a holiday 'in a place where there's nothing to eat'. The collapse of the Russian army in Persia left a vacuum and it was possible for the Germans to march in. The British feared that the Germans and the Turks would then be able to establish a route to Kabul and with Afghan help invade India. The enemy had to be stopped in the north before it could penetrate Persia, so British troops were sent out from Baghdad.

The Russian collapse in Persia, and then in Armenia, enabled the Turks to move troops from there down to Mosul and northern Mesopotamia. But British troops advanced up the Euphrates, and in March had a resounding victory over the Turks at Hit. Gertrude told her parents:

We have had a great *coup* up the Euphrates and annihilated the Turks there. . . . I think that will about end the war here.

The war in Mesopotamia was not over but its outcome was inevitable. However in the main theatre of war, on the Western front, the struggle was unremitting and the Allies uncertain of success.

In February 1918, despite censorship, Gertrude informed her parents of official telegrams concerning preparations for a 'terrific assault in France'. This so-called 'Great Battle' began with a massive German offensive on March 21. A few days later she wrote to her parents:

> One feels one can't look a fortnight ahead while this awful struggle is going on in France. I woke this morning with a sudden realisation of what an overwhelming disaster it would be if the Germans broke through. And if they don't how long will it last and how much will they feel the exhaustion of it?

At this time Gertrude was under considerable pressure from her father to return to England in the summer. She longed to see her family but dreaded going back as it would be 'so difficult to pick up life in England'. It was also difficult during war-time to obtain permission to travel along the Mediterranean but Gertrude's father had influence! And although Sir Percy Cox, on a visit to England, had persuaded Sir Hugh Bell of the difficulties of such a journey, Gertrude recognised that her father could

> always get me home by making the India office or the F O telegraph that they want me and asking the Admiralty to give me facilities.

While Sir Percy Cox was in England the deputy civil commissioner, Captain Arnold T. Wilson, took over. Gertrude found him 'a very remarkable creature' but admits they first distrusted each other: 'He began by regarding me as "a born intriguer" and I, not unnaturally regarded him with some suspicion also'. But in April she maintained that 'we have ended by becoming firm friends'. It was not a friendship that would last — she constantly undermined his authority and began to look very much 'a born intriguer'. She had already shown complete disregard for any rules of secrecy when corresponding with her parents and had maintained direct communication with Whitehall, ignoring the authority of her chief, the civil commissioner. And that correspondence with Whitehall would soon contain political views directly conflicting with those of her chief.

Despite continuing troubles in Persia Gertrude decided to spend her summer holidays there and on the way back to Baghdad learnt that Sir Percy was being sent to Tehran to negotiate an Anglo-Persian treaty although the British were still waging a substantial campaign in southern Persia. A. T. Wilson was now confirmed as Gertrude's chief.

Gertrude returned from her travels with strong views on developments in Persia. She was soon complaining to her parents:

> If it were not for the Persian enterprise, which I consider folly
> — and I've been and seen, which the War Office hasn't — we
> should now be launching our attack on Mosul. . .if we could
> have got up to Mosul we should have secured the great
> wheat-bearing area of the Arbela plain. . . . There are a number of other, smaller, political problems which also would have
> been settled, to say nothing of the fact that a striking success
> both in Syria and here must, I think, have knocked the Turks
> out.

Gertrude did not merely voice these grievances to her parents but also sent a personal letter directly to Lord Hardinge — that could scarcely have pleased her new chief, A. T. Wilson.

Despite Gertrude's misgivings about War Office policy it was only a matter of days before Syria collapsed under the pressure of Allenby's successes on its Palestine front. Damascus fell to the British on 1 October, and within a few days Tyre was taken and Beirut seized by the French. On 3 October Gertrude wrote: 'We are daily awaiting the news that Turkey is suing for peace. The Syrian campaign has been nothing short of a miracle'.

At exactly this time there had also been major military successes on the Western front, and on 4 October the Kaiser sent a first peace offer to the American president, Woodrow Wilson. On 11 November an armistice was signed with the Germans. Two weeks earlier an armistice had been signed with Turkey. The Great War was over. Now began the task of deciding the future of the conquered peoples. In Mesopotamia Gertrude felt herself in a strong position to exercise influence over the future of that country, and indeed she was. But first a short holiday for her on the banks of the Tigris. She records:

> A few days before I left Baghdad we had a wonderfully moving
> function whereat the C in C read to the public his proclamation
> on the declaration of the armistice with Turkey. The square
> was crowded with troops and notables; men and boys had
> climbed into the trees and were standing in the galleries of the

minarets. When the C in C had finished a sailor broke the flag on the big flagstaff in the centre of the square. We wrote the heading to a new chapter that day and I wondered what my Moslem friends were thinking.

9 Arab Affairs

On 7 November 1918, just ten days after the signing of the
Turkish armistice, the British and the French governments issued
a joint declaration concerning the future of the occupied Arab
territories, stating their aims to be:

> The complete and final enfranchisement of the peoples so long
> oppressed by the Turks, and the establishment of national
> governments and administrations drawing their authority from
> the initiative and free choice of native populations.

The Sharif of Mecca immediately saw this declaration as support
for his rule of Arab kingdoms — kingdoms he had been promised
for his cooperation with the Allies during the First World War.
Fervent support for the Sharifian cause came from Colonel T. E.
Lawrence who immediately put the Sharif's claims before A. T.
Wilson, who was acting high commissioner in Sir Percy's absence
in Persia. Wilson reacted strongly and instantly proposed that

> Sir Percy Cox should be appointed High Commissioner for the
> first five years without any Arab Amir or other head of State,
> but with Arab Ministers backed by British Advisers.

Furthermore Wilson suggested holding a plebiscite to assess
public opinion in Iraq.

Gertrude gave Wilson complete support in his views on the
future administration of Iraq. She wrote home from Baghdad in
late November 1918:

> The Franco–British Declaration has thrown the whole town
> into a ferment. It doesn't happen often that people are told that
> their future as a State is in their hands and asked what they
> would like. . . . On two points they are practically all agreed,
> they want us to control their affairs and they want Sir Percy as
> High Commissioner. Beyond that all is divergence. Most of the
> town people want an Arab Amir but they can't fix upon the
> individual. My belief is (but I don't yet know) that the tribal

people in the rural districts will not want any Amir so long as they can have Sir Percy — he has an immense name among them — and personally I think that would be best.

Indeed the plebiscite seemed to vindicate Wilson's expectations. There was certainly no popular surge of support for a Sharifian Amir in Iraq where the Sharifians were virtually unknown. And the large tribal Shi'a populations were very suspicious of any move to appoint a Sunni Muslim as Amir. But that was far from being the end of the matter: the Sharifian cause would soon gain voluble support from influential Arabists — like Gertrude Bell!

On 27 December 1918 Gertrude wrote unequivocally about her views on Arab rule:

In Mesopotamia they want us and no one else, because they know we'll govern in accordance with the custom of the country. They realise that an Arab Amir is impossible because, though they like the idea in theory, in practice they could never agree as to the individual.

But by the end of 1919 her ideas underwent a revolution. In early October she had visited Syria where the Sharif's eldest son Faisal had been allowed by the British to proclaim an independent Arab government despite French claims to parts of Syria. An area of French interest was recognized but Faisal was established with territorial and military authority, he could fly the Sharifian flag and claim to administer Syria on behalf of King Husain, his father. But it was Allenby, the British commander-in-chief who exercised supreme authority over all the occupied territory and acted as an intermediary between Faisal and the French representative.

When Gertrude returned she wrote in her report *Syria in October 1919* about the disorder and mismanagement of Sharifian rule in Syria but concluded:

It is true that the Arab administration has left much to be desired, and equally true that it has been artificially financed by our subsidy to the Sharif; but it has presented, nevertheless, the outward appearance of a national government . . . and if it crumbles . . . its failure will be attributed, not to inherent

defects, but to British indifference and French ambition . . . .
We have stated that it is our intention to assist and establish in
Syria and in Mesopotamia indigenous governments and admin-
istrations . . . I believe that events of the last year have left us no
choice in Mesopotamia.

Within a few months she was suggesting Faisal's brother as Amir
of Iraq:

Abdullah is a gentleman who likes a copy of the *Figaro* every
morning at breakfast time. I haven't any doubt we should get
on with him famously.

Soon it was Faisal himself who became Gertrude's own favourite
as king of an independent Iraq. And as with everything else, she
pursued this latest idea with an obsessive commitment that
would allow nothing to stand in her way.

But why the sudden turn around? Did her two-week visit to
Syria in October really change her whole perception of the
political problems of Iraq? I think not. She had already formed,
much earlier in the year, a strong political alliance with close
friends who were supporters of the Sharifian cause. Indeed it was
surely these friends — David Hogarth and T.E. Lawrence — who
finally won her complete sympathy for the Sharif and his heirs.

It was in March 1919, in Paris, that she met up with Lawrence
and Hogarth. Here, at the Conference of Paris, the Allied Powers
were framing treaties that would decide the territorial rights of
the Great War's victors and vanquished. In March the conference turned its attention to the Middle East and in particular the
conflicting interests of France and Britain in Syria. The French
interpreted the Sykes–Picot agreement as granting them the
whole of Syria but there was angry opposition from Faisal to
French intervention in Syria. He threatened to respond with a
huge war, supported even by the Arabs of the Hejaz. The British
were convinced that to maintain peace in the Middle East,
French ambitions in the region must be contained.

The British prime minister, Lloyd George, felt that an international commission to Syria, with British, French and American
delegates, would sort out the problem. The British working in the
Middle East knew that this would only unsettle Syria and alien-

ate Faisal. A lobby gathered in Paris to protect Faisal's position in Syria.

A.T. Wilson sent Gertrude to the Paris Conference in March, 1919 to explain the political problems of Iraq and to support the position of Faisal and the British in Syria. Wilson was far from being a supporter of the Sharifian cause and would not have sent Gertrude as a representative to the conference if she held strong views on that subject. But as a result of experiences at the conference her views would change.

The future of Iraq (as Mesopotamia came to be called after the war) was closely linked with that of Syria, and none of the British in the Middle East, including A.T. Wilson, wanted any French encroachment in Syria. Anything that would unsettle the Arabs of Syria would make life impossible for the British administration in Iraq. Gertrude went to join the lobby opposing Lloyd George's proposal for an international commission to Syria.

On arriving in Paris she wrote:

> I'm lunching tomorrow with Mr. Balfour [Foreign Secretary] who, I fancy, really doesn't care. Ultimately I hope to catch Mr Lloyd George by the coat tails, and if I can manage to do so I believe I can enlist his sympathies. Meantime we've sent for Colonel Wilson from Baghdad and Mr Hogarth from Cairo — the latter at my instigation — and when they come I propose to make a solid bloc of Near Easterns, including Mr Lawrence, and present a united opinion.

She also recorded that she spent most of her time at the conference with T. E. Lawrence. He was the most fervent supporter of the Sharifian's claims to Syria and Iraq, and he was no friend of Gertrude's chief A. T. Wilson — indeed a few months later Lawrence was appealing to Lord Curzon to remove Wilson from his post in Baghdad. Certainly Gertrude would never have allied herself with Wilson against her 'beloved boy' Lawrence. She never forgot Wilson's first description of her as a 'born intriguer' — the two would inevitably be on opposing sides of the Sharifian debate.

In Paris Lawrence was strongly supported by David Hogarth — who was of course also Gertrude's friend and mentor. Indeed Lawrence described Hogarth as '*Mentor* to all of us. . .our father confessor and adviser'. Lawrence and Hogarth had been friends since their Oxford days; they had worked together in archaeological enterprises before 1914 and during the war championed the Sharifian cause. Lawrence testified to the influence Hogarth exercised over the younger members of the Arab Bureau in Cairo. Surely it was not difficult in March 1919 for Lawrence and Hogarth to influence Gertrude Bell.

Lawrence must have rejoiced to win over Wilson's own oriental secretary. But Gertrude's new-found cause would lead her into terrible conflict with her chief and almost ended her career in Iraq.

Gertrude's *Syria in October 1919* report was her first official declaration of her Sharifian sympathies. It was sent, as were all her other reports, to the 'high and mighty' in Whitehall. But it was accompanied by a covering note from A. T. Wilson which explained his own conflicting views. He felt it impossible to create in Iraq 'a new sovreign Mohammedan State', and he pointed to the difficulty of placing a national government over the disparate groups living within the borders of Iraq — there were substantial Jewish and Christian minorities; the Shia numbered 1¾ million; there were half a million warlike Kurds, and he added that 'no form of Government has yet been envisaged, which does not involve Sunni domination'.

But the Foreign Office had already been wooed by supporters of the Sharifian cause, especially of course by T. E. Lawrence. And within the Foreign Office there was Sir Hubert Young giving strong support for Sharifian claims. He was responsible for dealing with middle-eastern questions and in November 1919 recorded that he was 'convinced that an immediate change was required in the spirit of our administration in Mesopotamia'. This view was impressed on the Foreign Secretary, Lord Curzon, who became 'seriously alarmed'.

By December 1919 it was clear that there were plans for Sir Percy Cox to return from Tehran and replace A. T. Wilson. But Sir Percy did not arrive in Baghdad until June 1920 and then he went directly to London for four months' negotiations on British policy in Mesopotamia. So Sir Percy did not fully assume his position as High Commissioner in Baghdad until October 1920. But during those four months he spent in London Gertrude felt thankful that he will be there to appeal to. For I can write everything to him as I can do to no one else, he being my real Chief, and he will be able to take direct action.

There was at this time a complete breakdown between Wilson and Gertrude. She ignored his authority completely, and continually communicated directly with his superiors. Wilson had complained to Sir Percy for months of Gertrude's unreliability and wrote in 'March of his intention to dismiss her in April. Sir Percy persuaded Wilson to retain her and perhaps ease the tension by allowing her leave for the hot season.

The hot season arrived and Gertrude did not take any leave — she was not going to allow herself to be gently squeezed out of Iraq. But she made no effort to improve her relationship with Wilson. In June she described 'an apalling scene last week with AT':

> I gave one of our Arab friends here a bit of information I ought not technically have given. It wasn't of much importance, and it didn't occur to me I had done wrong until I mentioned it casually . . . . He told me my indiscretions were intolerable and that I should never see another paper in the office. I apologised for that particular indiscretion . . . but he continued: "You've done more harm here than anyone. If I hadn't been going away myself I should have asked for your dismissal months ago — you and your Amir." I know really what's at the bottom of it — I've been right and he has been wrong.

But by July Wilson was writing directly to the India Office:

> If you can find a job for Miss Bell at home I think you will be well advised to do so. Her irresponsible activities are a source of considerable concern to me here and are not a little resented by the Political Officers.

Gertrude's dismissal was never likely — she enjoyed the support and confidence of highly-placed friends throughout Whitehall. However Wilson did succeed in restricting her access to confidential papers, but when he was replaced by Sir Percy in October Gertrude was once more taken into the confidence of her chief 'on matters of importance!'

Wilson had felt especially in need of loyalty from all members of his staff during the four months Sir Percy was in England. It was a time of unprecedented disturbances among the tribes on the Euphrates and there was mounting pressure back in England for complete withdrawal from Mesopotamia. Wilson needed to present a strong, united administration to the Arabs before the whole country succumbed to revolt.

The tribal troubles seem to have begun soon after the British government announced in May 1920 its acceptance, from the League of Nations, of a mandate over Iraq. The term 'mandate' itself caused considerable misunderstanding among the Arabs. But the main source of trouble for the British came from the religious leaders of the Shi'a. Gertrude explained that there was virtually no contact with 'the grimly devout citizens of the holy towns and more especially the leaders of religious opinion, the Mujtahids'. They were all 'bitterly pan-Islamic' and 'anti-British'. It was among these extremists that fervent nationalism began to bubble over in early June. Gertrude wrote home.

We have had a stormy week. The Nationalist propaganda increases. There are constant meetings in mosques . . . . The extremists are out for independence, without a mandate. They play for all they are worth on the passions of the mob and what with the Unity of Islam and the Rights of the Arab Race they make a fine figure. They have created a reign of terror.

To reassure the more moderate nationalists, the British announced on 20 June that Sir Percy Cox would return in October to establish a provisional Arab government and call an assembly, freely elected by the people, in consultation with which he would prepare an organic law. But by then nothing would have satisfied the extremist leaders and on 20 July the turbulent Shi'a tribes, encouraged by their religious leaders, broke into open revolt. The promises of the British government did nothing to assuage their fears of Sunni dominance.

The British immediately drafted reinforcements from India to suppress the revolt and Wilson issued orders 'forbidding the holding of meetings in Mosques, together with a curfew — no one to be out in the streets after 10 pm'. The revolt was stemmed but the British were forced to withdraw their political service from the Euphrates area; Gertrude commented: 'It's a sad business to see the whole organisation crumble'. It was not until February 1921 that the Arab rising was completely quelled.

Sir Percy Cox arrived in Baghdad in October 1920 committed to 'a complete and necessarily rapid transformation of the facade of the existing administration from British to Arab'. He found that 'not a few of the British element were sceptical as to the likelihood of the new enterprise succeeding and did not disguise their feelings'. His position was 'a very solitary one to begin with' but he enlisted the help of two allies 'Gertrude Bell and Mr Philby'. Of Gertrude, Sir Percy wrote that she 'had all the personnel and politics of the local communities at her fingers' end' and he continued:

I knew that her own ideas. . .on the subject of Arab aspirations were such that I could be sure that at any rate in principle they were heart and soul in sympathy with the present policy of government.

Sir Percy was quick to realise the value of Gertrude's local contacts and she was repeatedly sent to Arab notables as an intermediary to persuade them to cooperate in the formation of a provisional Arab government. In late October, soon after Sir Percy's return to Baghdad, he sent Gertrude to persuade Sasun Effendi Heskail — a well-respected leading member of the Baghdad Jewish community — to become finance minister in the new Council of State. She 'set off feeling as if I carried the future of all Iraq in my hands'. After an hour's intense argument with the reluctant Sasun she left with 'an inner conviction that the game was won — partly, thank heaven, to the relations of trust and confidence which I had personally already established with Sasun'.

Within a few days Sir Percy, with Gertrude's and Philby's help, had assembled a provisional government. Gertrude gave a dinner party for three of the most prominent members of the new council, all personal friends of hers: Sasun Effendi; Jafar Pasha, a celebrated and respected general; and Abdul Majd Shawi, mayor of Baghdad. Feeling the prowess of achievement, she wrote:

Long life to the Arab Government. Give them responsibility and make them settle their own affa rs and they'll do it every time a thousand times better than w2 can.

There is no doubt that Gertrude had real talent for making friends and influencing people. Sir Percy recognized the immense contribution she could make in setting up a new regime and channelled her energies in that direction. But Gertrude's political judgement was certainly not to be trusted. She confessed in early 1921, when considering Britain's political future in Iraq, that she was 'often wrong in prophecy'. Indeed as early as 1912 there was Cromer's letter to Curzon (see p. 52) explaining that although Gertrude was 'an extremely clever woman . . . she has not got much judgment'. Even when dealing with the Arab notables of Baghdad, whom she knew so intimately, her judgement was sometimes surprisingly poor. When Sir Percy received the widespread view that the Naqib (chief noble and head of the Sunni community in Baghdad) should be selected for presiding over the new Council of State, Gertrude had a clear opinion on the viability of this choice: 'I am convinced not only that the Naqib will refuse for himself, but that he will also refuse to recommend anyone'. A few days later the Naqib was approached by Sir Percy and accepted the appointment.

It is worth recalling that stunning example of her lack of judgement, cited in the last chapter, when she complained of War Office policy in managing the middle-eastern campaign during the First World War. One day she was writing directly to Lord Hardinge explaining that the present campaign would not succeed in conquering Syria or disabling the Turks. A few days later not only Syria but the whole Ottoman Empire collapsed and the war was over!

Fortunately for Gertrude Sir Percy shared her pro-Sharifian views; he did not tolerate dissent among his close political officers. Indeed within a year of Cox's arrival in Baghdad in 1920 he dismissed the talented Philby when he attempted to promote his protégé Sayyid Talib as the future ruler of Iraq. However Gertrude's choice for Amir found favour with Sir Percy. By the end of 1920 her earlier enthusiasm for Abdullah had shifted to the Sharif's eldest son, Faisal, who was already king in Syria:

I feel quite clear in my own mind that there is only one workable solution, a son of the Sharif and for choice Faisal: very very much the first choice.

Despite Gertrude's support for a national Arab government she did have misgivings about how it would take control over the different factions living within the borders of Iraq. And as the new year 1921 arrived she reflected:

I don't think I ever woke on a first of January with such feelings of apprehension. . . . For the truth is there's little that promises well.

The distrust between Sunni and Shi'a was at the root of her apprehension:

I hear rumours that the Sunnis of Baghdad are considering whether it wouldn't suit their book best to have a Turkish prince as King. They are afraid of being swamped by the Shiahs, against whom a Turk might be a better bulwark than a son of the Sharif. The present Government which is predominantly Sunni, isn't doing anything to conciliate the Shiahs. They are now considering a number of administrative appointments for the provinces; almost all the names they put up are Sunnis, even for the wholly Shiah province on the Euphrates . . . I believe if we could put up a son of the Sharif he might yet sweep the board; if we hesitate, the tide of public opinion may turn overwhelmingly to the Turks.

Gertrude did not have much sympathy with Shi'a complaints of lack of representation and told Domnul that they were 'wholly overlooking the fact that nearly all their leading men are Persian subjects and must change their nationality before they can hold office in the Mesopotamian State'.

Gertrude's former chief A. T. Wilson had early recognized the problems that Sunni–Shi'a tension posed in Iraq:

The population is so deeply divided by racial and religious cleavages, and the Shiah majority after two hundred years of Sunni domination are so little accustomed to hold high office that any attempt to introduce institutions, on the lines desired by the advanced Sunni politicians of Syria, would involve the concentration of power in the hands of a few persons whose ambitions and methods would rapidly bring about the collapse of organised government.

For Wilson it spelled disaster for any attempt to be made to set up a national government in Iraq. Even as late as June 1920 he was still advocating re-establishment of the Ottoman Empire which he saw as 'the embodiment of the Muslim ideal of temporal rule on earth'. His views did not find sympathy with the British government and seriously undermined Britain's position in Iraq. What was needed was united and decisive action from the British — and many British believed that the exact nature of that action was less important than its swift and determined implementation. Gertrude blamed much of Iraq's instability, especially the revolt of the lower Euphrates tribes, on Wilson's 'short-sighted vision', and at the close of 1920 described him as 'having done as much harm as any individual could do'. Indeed he himself admitted a decade later that he had 'underestimated the influence of the Nationalists'.

Although Gertrude viewed 1921 with gloom the British government was poised to act in a united and decisive way in the Middle East. Early in 1921 Iraq policy decisions were transferred from the India Office to the Colonial Office where the Secretary of State was Winston Churchill. He immediately summoned a conference at Cairo to discuss the future of the Middle East. In March 1921 Sir Percy Cox went to the conference accompanied by his Oriental Secretary.

Gertrude approached the conference with strong misgivings suspecting there would be pressure for a Turkish prince to be made Amir. She also feared that her own and Sir Percy's absence from Iraq would enable the forces of disruption to gain ground. Indeed she had at first been reluctant to go with Sir Percy to Cairo. She felt

so anxious at leaving the country to itself during his absence that on the whole I think it would be better for me to stay here, for as far as anyone can do anything to shape public opinion, I believe I'm one of the people who can.

The whole of Iraq was unsettled by the uncertainties of the impending Cairo conference. Gertrude also noted that

> the French are, I suspect, up to their usual dirty tricks. Izzat Pasha tells me that he knows for certain they are stirring up the Kurds not to come in with Iraq but to ask for a French mandate.

Gertrude arrived in Cairo on 12 March and immediately met up with T. E. Lawrence while 'Sir Percy was closeted with Mr. Churchill'.

Within a fortnight she was returning to Baghdad delighted with the results of the conference. She and Sir Percy had presented 'a definite programme' for Iraq which 'coincided exactly with that which the Secretary of State had brought with him'. The doubts that preceded the conference disappeared and now she could 'feel certain that we shall have the current nationalist opinion in our favour and I've no doubt of success'.

Plans were made for Faisal to visit Iraq. He was the conference's choice for Amir but they agreed there would be an election in Iraq to assess the extent of popular support for him. Gertrude had no doubt of the success of Faisal's election and decided not to visit England in summer 1921 as the new Amir 'will need a great deal of help and guidance and its more than I could bear not to be there to give whatever hand I can'.

Faisal arrived in Basra in June 1921 and reached Baghdad two weeks later. He was baffled by the reports he had received as he travelled along the Euphrates. Gertrude explained that 'all the way up the story they had heard was, the High Commissioner is neutral, the Khatun and Mr. Garbett want Faisal and Mr. Philby wants a republic'. But once in Baghdad Gertrude 'assured him Sir Percy was absolutely with him'. Soon after, Philby's position became untenable and he was forced to resign.

Immediately after Faisal's arrival in Baghdad Gertrude assumed the role of his adviser. She took it upon herself to brief him before his first discussions with Sir Percy. Gertrude was sure that Faisal would sweep the country in an election; she wrote: 'We've

At the Cairo Conference, 1921. Gertrude Bell (on the camel in front of the Sphinx) has Winston Churchill on her right.

got Baghdad and I'm pretty certain we've got Mosul; the rest will fall into line.' But she was forced to recognize that there were still troubles among the lower Euphrates tribes where she heard of preparations of 'monstrous petitions in favour of a republic and of Shiah Alim Mutjahids being all against Faisal', but she insisted that 'somehow or other Faisal must be proclaimed King'.

It soon became clear to the British administration that a formal election procedure would take too long — it would be months before an electoral register could be completed. The British realized how important it was to create the appearance of Faisal being swept to power in a surge of popular enthusiasm; keeping him lingering in the side wings for months of uncertainty would do nothing for his prestige or that of the British. So it was decided in July to hold a country-wide referendum, the result of which would be known in just four weeks. During these weeks Sir Percy Cox and Faisal began to establish a new Sharifian party — this would be the political power base supporting Faisal's authority. Moderate Arab opinion was channelled into this new party and Faisal was sent round the country canvassing support. He was sent to the Sunni tribesmen of the Euphrates and introduced to the notable Christians and Jews in Baghdad. The whole campaign was carefully orchestrated by the British and always at hand was Gertrude, introducing him to the people 'we thought he ought to speak to'.

By early August the referendum was completed and claimed 96 per cent support for Faisal as king of Iraq. This percentage is somewhat incredible, for there were such large numbers conspicuously opposed to him — the extreme Shi'a and the whole Kurdish population. But the British felt they had succeeded in sweeping him to power and stabilizing the political situation in Iraq. Before the end of August 1921 Faisal was crowned king.

Gertrude had worked relentlessly to secure Faisal the throne of Iraq but she was exhausted by the effort and declared she would 'never engage in creating kings again; it's too great a strain'. Gertrude was not only intent on creating the king but also his court. She insisted Faisal's wife should take her proper place — not as a protected and retiring wife of a great sheikh, but as that of a queen, European-style. Gertrude also insisted on the practice of curtsying to the king, but found the other British womenfolk resentful about adopting this formality with an elected king.

Every detail of the new court fell under Gertrude's scrutiny: she took great care in designing the new Sharifian flag for Iraq and wrote to her father asking him to telegraph her as to whether her suggestion was 'heraldically right'; she also discussed with Faisal 'the founding of a Mesopotamian order (for we must have a decoration of our own)'. And throughout 1922 and 1923 she assumed responsibility for furnishing Faisal's palace, ordering furniture from the London store Waring and Gillow.

Gertrude adored Faisal. She wrote of his 'fine dignity' and his 'splendid' appearance in 'white robes with a fine black abba over them, flowing white headdress and silver bound Aqal'. Her descriptions read as if they belong to an eastern fairy-tale with a handsome prince riding out of the desert to take his place on the throne of Iraq with his chief adviser, Gertrude, at his side. She was enchanted by Faisal and admitted to her father that 'I sometimes think I must be in a dream'.

Faisal's coronation in August 1921 did not bring as swift and peaceful rule to Iraq as the British had hoped. There was continuing unrest caused by Turkish attacks in the north and Ibn Sa'ud was stirring up trouble in the desert to the south-west. Also relations between the British and Iraq governments were tense. By early 1922 the king and his ministers made it clear that they would not accept any sort of mandatory relations with Britain; instead they insisted on a simple treaty of alliance. Gertrude saw it as inevitable that the mandate would have to be dropped, but during the treaty negotiations she played no part — in December 1921 she wrote to her father:

> But you mustn't think for a moment I have any part in settling these problems. I know about them because Sir Percy tells me about them in outline but I'm a mere onlooker and although Faisal is very friendly and agreeable he doesn't, quite rightly, consult me.

The Arab regime she had worked so hard to establish in Iraq was now making its own decisions and Gertrude's political role was dissipating fast. In October 1921 she wrote despondently: 'I think I may have been of some use here but I suspect I've come very near the end of it'. But she was soon establishing new responsibilities in Iraq.

Archaeology had always been a prime interest for Gertrude. There were plans for a considerable Anglo-American expedition to dig at Ur. Gertrude was anxious that Iraq should not lose all its ancient treasures to foreign countries. And in July 1922 she obtained the king's support for a Law of Excavations which she had 'compiled with the utmost care in consultation with the legal authorities'. It allowed for a fifty-fifty share of discovered treasures between Iraq and the archaeologists. Faisal also accepted Gertrude's suggestion that he should appoint her as 'Provisional Director of Archaeology' to his government. Gertrude's new role as protector and preserver of Iraq's archaeological wealth was really a poor substitute for the political influence she once wielded. But by summer 1922 Gertrude's political involvement was negligible — Faisal no longer asked her advice and his own political manipulations to achieve his aims soon tarnished Gertrude's romantic image of him. And when, in the summer, she learnt of his support for 'the most ignoble extremists' she was devastated and went to tell the king how he was destroying all that she had worked for:

I began by asking him whether he believed in my personal sincerity and devotion to him. He said he could not doubt it. . .I said in that case I could speak with perfect freedom. . .I had formed a beautiful and gracious snow image to which I had given allegiance and I saw it melting before my eyes. Before every noble outline had been obliterated, I preferred to go; in spite of my love for the Arab nation and my sense of responsibility for its future, I did not think I could bear to see the evaporation of the dream which had guided me day by day.

Faisal explained that he was only trying to reassure the extremists, and at the end of the meeting Gertrude declared Faisal to be 'one of the most lovable of human beings; but he is amazingly lacking in strength of character'. In fact Faisal showed considerable political nerve in his dealings with Britain.

The negotiations with Britain finally produced a treaty of alliance which was signed on 10 October 1922. But ratification was delayed. The coalition government in Britain, under which the treaty had been framed and signed, resigned on 23 October and the question of the future of Iraq became an issue in the general election campaign. There was a move in the British press supporting complete and immediate withdrawal from Iraq so that it would no longer be a drain on the British treasury. The uncertainty of Iraq's future was exploited by the Turks who laid claim to the very large Mosul vilayet in Iraq and by January 1923 they were massing troops on Iraq's northern frontier.

Despite the unsettled state of Iraq and fears of a Turkish invasion and the return of Turkish rule, Faisal made preparations in October 1922 for elections. He wanted an Assembly set up by early 1923 so that it could, among other things, promptly ratify the Treaty of Alliance with Britain.

In January 1923 Sir Percy Cox returned to England to help influence Cabinet policy on Iraq. Gertrude explained to her father:

> It is far more satisfactory that he in person should go and put the whole case to the authorities, for you see, even if they don't want to shoulder the burden they have got to learn that it's amazingly difficult to let it drop with a bump. Even the evacuation of Mosul would mean, I am convinced, that we should be faced with the problem of sixty or seventy thousand Christian refugees.

The king's plans for prompt elections quickly ran into considerable obstacles, notably from the Shi'a religious leaders who issued a decree forbidding the elections to take place. By summer 1923 Faisal was forced to authorize deportation of the chief obstructionist among the Shi'a divines, Sheikh Mahdi al Khalisi. He was followed to Persia by a number of other religious leaders, and the election procedure went forward with no further disruption.

Gertrude spent the summer of 1923 back in England. It was her first return home for more than three years but she only stayed for a few weeks and was back in Iraq in August because 'the elections are coming on and the people want help and guidance'.

She returned to Baghdad as Oriental Secretary to Sir Henry Dobbs. Her former and much-loved chief, Sir Percy Cox, had retired a few months earlier. She sorely missed him:

We had worked together on and off for six years, and through difficult times. It had become a habit that he should always want to talk things over with me. Sir Henry doesn't always do that — often he does the thing first and then tells me about it.

Gertrude continued to write intelligence reports and lengthy articles on the political situation in Iraq but she was no longer at the heart of developments — more an observer and reporter. Her influence was now confined to the field of archaeology where she closely supervised the division of spoils between the archaeologists and Iraq. But her interest in the affairs of state remained keen and she wrote home long letters describing every nuance of each political development.

At the end of February 1924 she wrote excitedly that 'the sensation of the week is the elections, the results of which are coming out daily. Baghdad was declared on Monday. On the whole very good and such other reports as are in are good too.' By mid-March all the election results were declared and the new Constituent Assembly was opened by the king on 27 March.

The most important matter on the Assembly's agenda was the Treaty of Alliance with Britain. There had been extensive negotiations with Britain to try and improve the terms of the Treaty especially those involving finance. Faisal insisted that Iraq could not possibly sustain the financial burden Britain was inflicting — not only was Iraq required to expand substantially its army and redeem the capital cost of the railways but also assume a large share of the inherited Ottoman Debt. Britain did yield and agreed to reconsider these financial matters after the Treaty was ratified and to ensure that happened quickly Britain gave the Assembly until midnight on 10 June to accept the Treaty or it would be assumed it had been rejected. Any apparent rejection of the Treaty would have been a disaster for Faisal. On 11 June Gertrude noted that 'we beat Cinderella by half an hour — the Treaty was ratified last night at 11.30'.

The ratification of the Treaty was only one of the three conditions that Churchill, in the spring of 1921 at the Cairo conference, had insisted must be fulfilled before Britain would move towards terminating its mandatory relations with Iraq. The other two were the introduction of an Electoral and Organic Law and the establishment of agreed frontiers. The laws were passed by the new Assembly in August 1924. But there were immense difficulties in establishing undisputed frontiers in the south-west with Ibn Sa'ud and in the north with the Turks.

Ibn Sa'ud's followers continued to raid Iraq shepherd tribes throughout 1924 and 1925, but agreement was finally reached with Ibn Sa'ud in late 1925. The frontier with Turkey was much more of a problem and the League of Nations sent a Frontier Commission to Iraq in January 1925. A few days after its arrival in Baghdad Gertrude observed that: 'If good comes out of the Frontier Commission it will be mainly due to Sir Henry's extraordinarily tactful handling and the charming courtesy with which he and Esme [his wife] have treated them'. Such is the nature of diplomacy!

The Commission travelled to the disputed territory of Mosul and issued a report in August 1925 stating that if all the Mosul vilayet was contained with Iraq, as was the popular local demand, then Britain must maintain mandatory relations with Iraq for twenty-five years instead of the four which had been agreed in the existing Treaty of Alliance. The Treaty was rewritten and included a provision for the termination of mandatory relations whenever Iraq became a member of the League of Nations.

On 3 October 1932 Iraq was voted admission to the League of Nations. The High Commissioner became the British Ambassador; the mandate ended; and Iraq was an independent state. But Gertrude did not live to see her dream fulfilled.

10 Last Years

Gertrude returned home to England for the summer of 1925. She arrived in July and was, as her stepmother later stated, 'in a condition of great nervous fatigue, and appeared exhausted mentally and physically'. The family doctor thought her in no condition to return to Baghdad. But Gertrude dreaded staying in England where she felt so out of place and wondered how she would fill all those empty hours that stretched before her. She posed the problem to Janet Courtney and her old friend suggested that Gertrude stand for Parliament — somewhat ironical in view of Gertrude's former involvement in the Anti-Suffrage League! Gertrude replied promptly:

> No I'm afraid you will never see me in the House. I have an invincible hatred of that kind of politics and if you knew how little I should be fitted for it you would not give it another thought . . . my natural desire is to slip back into the comfortable arena of archaeology and history and to take only an onlooker's interest in the contest over actual affairs . . . I think I must certainly go back [to Baghdad] for this winter, though I privately doubt whether it won't be the last.

And indeed it was to be her last winter in Baghdad.

England held the family she loved but Baghdad was her home and she rejoiced at returning there in October 1925:

> It has been so wonderful coming back here. For the first two days I could not do any work at all in the office, because of the uninterrupted streams of people who came to see me. "Light of our eyes," they said, "Light of our eyes," as they kissed my hands and made almost absurd demonstrations of delight and affection. It goes a little to the head, you know — I almost began to think I were a Person.

In Baghdad she was a 'Person', in England she was an oddity.

She continued her work as Sir Henry Dobbs's Oriental Secretary but it was for the most part routine work. And in May 1926

112

she began seriously to consider her future in Iraq, writing to her father:

> What I vaguely think of doing (but don't talk about it) is to stay with the High Commission till . . .the autumn; then resign and ask the Iraq Government to take me on as Director of Antiquities for six months or so. (I'm only Hon. Director now, you know.) I should not in any case stay much longer with the H.C.; it has really ceased to be my job. Politics are dropping out and giving place to big administrative questions in which I'm not concerned and at which I'm no good. On the other hand the Dept. of Antiquities is now a full time job.

Two months earlier she had been given a 'proper building' in Baghdad for a new museum of archaeology. Its repair preoccupied her through spring 1926 but by July it was ready:

> Now all the very valuable objects — they run into tens of thousands of pounds and incidentally they would never have been taken out of the ground if I had not been here to guarantee that they would be properly protected, have been transferred pellmell into the new building and there is absolutely no one but I who knows anything about them.

But she concluded this letter to her father with the reflection that 'except for the Museum work, life is very dull'.

She had few social engagements and most of her friends among the British administration had left Baghdad. One of the last to leave was the architect J.M. Wilson who had first arrived in Baghdad in 1918. When he left in November 1925 Gertrude wrote sadly: 'J.M. Wilson has gone — for good. . . I do miss him so much'.

There were occasional visitors from England and in February 1926 Vita Sackville-West arrived. Gertrude gave her dinner and took her to tea with Faisal. Vita had met Gertrude before in England but now she was much more impressed with her in Baghdad,

> in her right place, in her own house, with her office in the city, and her white pony in a corner of the garden, and her Arab

113

servants, and her English books, and her Babylonian shards on the mantlepiece, and her long thin nose, and her irrepressible vitality.

One of Gertrude's few remaining friends in Baghdad was Lionel Smith who had arrived there in about 1921 and was Adviser to the Minister of Education in the Iraq Cabinet. Before the First World War he had been Dean of Magdalen College, Oxford, and tutor to Edward VII. He was Gertrude's frequent companion on her tours of inspection of archaeological excavations in Iraq, and in the spring of 1926 they went off together to Ur, taking with them 'a Dante from which to read our favourite cantos'. As always Gertrude took over the organization of the trip, commenting:

> Lionel is the vaguest of travellers and what he does when he is by himself I can't think. . . . He admitted that he was much more comfortable when he travelled with me and found breakfast turn up when wanted.

By summer 1926 Lionel Smith was her only regular visitor. In June she wrote despondently to J.M. Wilson:

> Except for the museum, I am not enjoying life at all. One has the sharp sense of being near the end of things with no certainty as to what, if anything, one will do next. It is also very dull, but for the work. I don't know what to do with myself of an afternoon . . .Lionel often comes to tea and we walk together. . . . But it is a very lonely business living here now.

She told Wilson of her plans to return to England after the summer and stay there for good. But she also reflected on the sad state of her family and its fortunes. There had been a general strike in England during May; it was caused by a bitter coal strike which long outlasted it. The coal strike had a devastating impact on Bell industries, forcing the family during 1926 to abandon their cherished home at Rounton Grange because they could no longer afford its upkeep.

Gertrude's family pressed her to return to England, fearing that she could not withstand the strain of another exhausting

114

Baghdad summer. But for Gertrude it was Baghdad alone that still held the possibility of some fulfillment — through her work at the museum. And so she stayed. Clearly wearied by the heat she wrote shorter letters home, explaining in her last letter to her father on July 7: 'Summer does not conduce to the writing of very long letters'.

On 12 July in the early hours of the morning she died from an overdose of her prescribed sleeping potion.

Was it intent or accident that led to her taking a fatal dose of the barbiturate? Her closest remaining friend in Baghdad had no doubt: Lionel Smith told Vita Sackville-West that Gertrude had committed suicide. He explained she had taken her life because she knew herself to be ill. And indeed she was — too ill to carry on through the fierce Baghdad summer and too fearful of the emptiness she would find in England.

Baghdad would now forever remain her home.

Chronology

1868	14 July	Gertrude Margaret Lothian Bell born at Washington Hall, County Durham.
1883–6		At school at Queen's College, London.
1886	Spring (to)	At Lady Margaret Hall, University of
1888	June	Oxford; takes first class degree in modern history. Visits Lascelles in Romania. Meets Valentine Chirol, 'Domnul'.
1889–92		In England.
1892	May–Dec.	Visits Lascelles in Persia; meets and falls in love with Henry Cadogan.
1893	January	In Switzerland with Mary Talbot.
	April to summer	In Algiers with her father; to Switzerland, and then to Weimar to meet Maurice.
1896	April	In Italy with Mrs Norman Grosvenor and Mrs J. R. Green.
	May–Dec.	In England.
1897	Jan–March	Visits Lascelles in Berlin.
	August	Family trip to Dauphiné, France.
	Dec. (to)	Round with world with Maurice.
1898	June	
1899	Spring	Visits northern Italy; to Greece with her father; to Constantinople.
	August	Bayreuth for Wagner festival.
	Nov. (to)	Visit to Rosens in Jerusalem. First desert
1900	June	journeys: to Jebel Druze.
1901	Aug.–Sept.	Climbing in Switzerland.
1902	Jan.–May	Travels with her father to Malta, Sicily and Italy; alone to Asia Minor.
	July–Aug.	Climbing in Switzerland.
	Dec.(to)	Round the world with Hugo, including
1903	July	Delhi durbar.
1904	August	Climbing in Switzerland.
	November	In Paris studying with Reinach.
1905	Jan.–May	Through Syrian desert to Asia Minor; recorded in *Syria: The Desert and the Sown* (1907).

	October	In Paris studying with Reinach.
	Dec. (to)	Travels with father to Gibraltar, Tangiers,
1906	Spring	Spain, Paris. In England writing *The Desert and the Sown*.
1907	Jan.–Feb.	Visits Cairo with her father.
	April–Aug.	Asia Minor: archaeological work with Sir William Ramsay. First meeting with Doughty-Wylie.
1908		In England writing *A Thousand and One Churches* (1909).
	July	Founder member of Woman's Anti-Suffrage League.
1909	Feb.–April	Travels in Syrian desert; visits Ukhaidir.
	Summer	In England working on *The Palace and Mosque at Ukhaidir* (1913).
1910	February	Italy; Germany.
1911	Jan.–June	Syrian desert; Ukhaidir; Babylon, Baghdad, Tur Abdin; Carchemish — first meeting with T. E. Lawrence.
1912		In England.
1913	Nov. (to)	Journey to Ha'il — imprisoned there.
1914	May	
	Nov. (to)	Boulogne, working in Red Cross Office.
1915	Feb.	
	March–Nov.	London, Red Cross Office.
	Nov. (to)	Working with Military Intelligence, Cairo.
1916	Jan.–Feb.	India — visit to Viceroy Hardinge.
	March (to)	Basrah — working for Sir Percy Cox.
1917	March	
	April (to)	Baghdad. Oct. 1917, awarded CBE
1919	Jan.	
	March	Paris Peace Conference.
	April	Motor tour through France with her father.
	May–July	England.
1921	February	Cairo Peace Conference.
	April (to)	Baghdad.
1925	June	
	July–Oct.	Holiday in England.
	Oct.	Returns to Baghdad.
1926	12 July	Dies in Baghdad.

Glossary

Amir	Title of Mohammedan ruler.
Bedouin	Arab of the desert.
Beg (or bey)	Turkish governor of a province or district.
Caliph	Mohammedan title of chief civil and religious leader; successor of Mohammed.
Druze	Political and religious sect of Mohammedan origin, living in region round Mount Lebanon.
Effendi	Turkish title of respect applied to officials and professional men.
Ghazu	Desert raid.
Kaimakam	In the Ottoman Empire a deputy governor of a province or district.
Keffiyeh	Cloth worn as head-dress by the Bedouin.
Kurds	Inhabitants of Kurdistan, with deep-rooted nationalist aspirations; mainly Sunnis of the Shafi'ite sect.
Naqib	Chief noble and head of Baghdad Sunni community
Pasha	Turkish title of officers of high rank, including military commanders and governors of provinces.
Sayyid	In Mohammedan countries a descendant of the Prophet through his elder grandson Husain.
Sheikh	Chief of an Arab family or tribe.
Shi'a	Name of Mohammedan sect which maintains that Ali (Mohammed's cousin and son-in-law) and his descendants were the true successor of the Prophet and regard the Sunni Caliphs as usurpers.
Sufi	A sect of Mohammedan ascetic mystics.
Sunni	Orthodox Muslims who accept not only the Koran but also the traditional teaching of Mohammed, or Sunna.
Vilayet	Province of the Turkish empire ruled by a vali or governor-general.
Wahabis	Sect originating in Arabia in the eighteenth century when Mohammed Wahab tried to restore the primitive form of Islam.

Select Bibliography

This bibliography is far from being an exhaustive list of all the works used in writing this biography. Only the most important are listed, including some general histories which are invaluable in understanding the world in which Gertrude Bell lived. Most of the books listed under 'Secondary Sources' can readily be obtained from any public library and many are available in paperback.

Primary Sources

Bell, F. (ed.) (1930), *The Letters of Gertrude Bell*, Benn, London.
Bell, G. (1928), *Persian Pictures*, Benn, London. First published anonymously in 1894 as *Safar Nameh. Persian Pictures*, Bentley, London.
—(1897), *Poems from the Divan of Hafiz*, Heinemann, London.
—(1907), *The Desert and The Sown*, Heinemann, London.
—(1909), with Sir William Ramsay, *The Thousand and One Churches*, Hodder and Stoughton, London.
—(1911), *Amurath to Amurath*, Heinemann, London.
—(1914), *Palace and Mosque at Ukhaidir*, Clarendon Press, Oxford.
—(1920), *Review of the Civil Administration of Mesopotamia*, Cmd. 1061, HMSO.
—(1926), 'Iraq: Political History' in *Encyclopaedia Britannica*, 13th ed.
Richmond, E. (ed.) (1937), *Earlier Letters of Gertrude Bell*, Benn, London.

Secondary Sources

Banks, J.A. and O. (1964), *Feminism and Family Planning in Victorian England*, Liverpool UP. Includes analysis of social changes among middle and upper-middle classes.
Black, E.C. (ed.) (1973), *Victorian Culture and Society*, Macmillan,

London. A rich collection of documents with editorial notes.

Briggs, A. (1971), *Victorian Cities*, Penguin Books, Harmondsworth. Contains a chapter on Middlesbrough which traces its development by the local industrialists, including the Bell family.

Burgoyne, E. (1958), *Gertrude Bell: From Her Personal Papers 1889–1914*, vol.1, Benn, London.

—(1961), *Gertrude Bell: From Her Personal Papers 1914–1926*, vol.2, Benn, London.

Courtney, Mrs W.L. [Janet Hogarth] (1926), *Recollected in Tranquillity*, London.

—(1931), *An Oxford Portrait Gallery*, London.

Fisher, S.N. (1971), *The Middle East*, Routledge and Kegan Paul, London.

Grenville, J.A.S. (1980), *A World History of the Twentieth Century:* vol.1, *Western Dominance, 1900–1945*, Fontana, London.

Harrison, B. (1978), *Separate Spheres*, Croom Helm, London. A detailed account of the anti-suffrage movement.

Kedourie, E. (1978), *England and the Middle East*, Harvester Press, Brighton. An especially helpful book on complicated negotiations, with details on some of the personalities involved.

Lewis, J. (1984), *Women in England 1870–1950: Sexual Divisions and Social Change*, Wheatsheaf Books, Brighton.

Roberts, J.M. (1970), *Europe 1880–1945*, Longman, London.

Webb, R.K. (1969), *Modern England: From the 18th Century to the Present*, Allen and Unwin, London.

Winstone, H.V.F. (1980), *Gertrude Bell*, Quartet, London.

—(1982), *The Illicit Adventure: The Story of Political and Military Intelligence in the Middle East from 1898 to 1926*, Cape, London.

Index